IMAGES
of America

REMEMBERING MAAS BROTHERS

IMAGES
of America

REMEMBERING
MAAS BROTHERS

Michael J. Lisicky
foreword by former Tampa mayor Sandy Freedman

ARCADIA
PUBLISHING

Copyright © 2015 by Michael J. Lisicky
ISBN 978-1-4671-1473-8

Published by Arcadia Publishing
Charleston, South Carolina

Printed in the United States of America

Library of Congress Control Number: 2015936189

For all general information, please contact Arcadia Publishing:
Telephone 843-853-2070
Fax 843-853-0044
E-mail sales@arcadiapublishing.com
For customer service and orders:
Toll-Free 1-888-313-2665

Visit us on the Internet at www.arcadiapublishing.com

CONTENTS

FOREWORD

Everybody has a story about Maas Brothers. We had a personal relationship with that downtown Tampa store. We knew the salespeople, and some of them took care of us and then took care of our children. I personally remember the makeup counter because it was the first place that I ever bought cosmetics. I had so many fond memories of that store. My father had a fine-jewelry store that was located across the street from the Tampa Theater. Maas Brothers was so much a part of my growing up, and I never heard anybody talk badly about it.

To this day, people still remember the cinnamon twists. We did not have these types of things in those days. Maas Brothers did the department store thing, but it also had this nice little restaurant. My father ate at Maas Brothers almost every day, and I remember going home many a day with a container of those cinnamon twists.

I had been to the St. Petersburg store, but it was not the same as the downtown Tampa location. I do not think that they considered it to be "their store" as we did with "our store" in Tampa. The downtown Tampa store was just a cozier space. Besides, Tampa is the center of the region, and it will always be the commercial hub. St. Petersburg has changed dramatically over the years, and it has now become a significantly younger community. But in the past, we were not nearly as mobile as we are now. We just did not have the road network. If you lived in Tampa, you did not need to shop in St. Petersburg and vice-versa.

Downtown Tampa eventually transitioned, and there was a huge flight to Westshore. But I stayed loyal to the downtown store until they closed their doors. There were always reasons to go there. Besides, I worked at city hall. In all fairness, there would not be the other stores if it were not for the Tampa store. It was the mother store.

— Sandy Freedman, former Tampa mayor

ACKNOWLEDGMENTS

I have learned that books such as these are not possible without the help of special people and archival institutions. Many photographs and pieces of Maas Brothers ephemera are still alive and maintained well under the care of the following people and organizations: David Parsons and the Tampa–Hillsborough County Public Library and Tampa Bay History Center, Ann Wikoff and the St. Petersburg Museum of History, Matthew Knight and the Special and Digital Collections at the University of South Florida, Adam Watson and the Florida State Archives Florida Memory Project, Kevin Logan at the Lakeland Public Library Special Collections Department, and the Manatee County Public Library Digital Collection. A message of deep appreciation goes to Lisa Lichtenberg, Richard Stein, Ron Rodriguez, Megan Weber, and Sue Meadows for sharing their own personal photographs. All of the above institutions and people are credited for their respective contributions. Any images that are not credited are part of my personal collection. I also must cite the great reference *Maas Brothers: The Tradition Continues*, compiled by Jeffrey E. Plourde. If you are a Maas Brothers fanatic, find it and read it.

In order to tell a story properly, you need memories and stories that will complement these images. A big thank-you goes to former Tampa mayor Sandy Freedman and the assistance of Debra Rotolo for her introductory thoughts and Audrey Maas Shine and all of the many Maas Brothers executives and employees who came forward and shared their experiences with this beloved institution. I cannot thank Lisa Lichtenberg enough for spearheading this effort. But I must also give special thanks to some people who answered my call and opened up their memories and contacts to me, especially Robert Stein, Ron Rodriguez, Chuck James, Ann Ruppert, Robert Walton, and Talbot Boudreau. Please enjoy reading their thoughts and those from many others throughout this book.

It is always comforting to know that I am not the only person who still holds these places close to my heart, for reasons that I cannot always explain. And it is comforting to know that I have a wife and daughter who are extremely patient and supportive of this obsession and passion.

This image, courtesy of Lisa Lichtenberg, is a collage of the people and places of Maas Brothers over the years.

INTRODUCTION

Only a handful of American cities were dominated solely by one classic department store. Columbus had Lazarus, Detroit had Hudson's, Miami had Burdines, Houston had Foley's, and Tampa had Maas Brothers.

The typical department-store rivalries simply did not exist in Tampa. There was no Macy's versus Gimbels feud. The dispute about Boston's "real" Santa Claus residing at Filene's or Jordan Marsh never occurred. The superiority of Pittsburgh's Kaufmann's or Joseph Horne's department-store restaurants was never debated.

Although there were other shopping options, Tampa did not necessarily need or want another major department store in its hometown. The Tampa community, and ultimately the entire region, depended on Maas Brothers for its shopping and social needs.

Over time, Maas Brothers developed into much more than a downtown Tampa institution. In 1948, the company opened a large streamlined operation in downtown St. Petersburg and became a part of that city's fabric and identity. Its success brought the Maas name to additional locations such as Lakeland, Sarasota, and Clearwater. By the 1970s, Maas Brothers was located throughout Florida's West Coast, but it never developed on the state's East Coast. The two coasts had separate identities with separate tastes. Florida was a big state with unique cities. Miami was not Tampa, and Tampa was not Jacksonville.

I always associated Maas Brothers with Tampa Bay, and vice-versa. The stores were not ostentatious. They had a distinctly casual atmosphere, much like the area's residents. When Burdines, Gayfers, Robinson's, and Ivey's came to the area, they were outsiders. These intruders tried to challenge Maas Brothers' dominance, but it was an uphill battle. It is not surprising; the Tampa Bay region was loyal to its hometown store.

Even to this day, many Tampa Bay residents mourn the loss of their favorite store. They are not alone. Most American cities have lost their favorite local store. In recent years, retail analysts have questioned the relevance of today's brick-and-mortar businesses. Stores have transitioned into showrooms, and a large number of retail transactions are now handled electronically.

When Maas Brothers closed, distinctive traditions ended. Tampa Bay shoppers could no longer purchase cinnamon twists, wait in long lines at the Blockbuster Sale in St. Petersburg, or call Jane Lee for shopping assistance. They could not spend a Saturday shopping on Franklin Street or have lunch in the Neptune Room, and there were no movies at the Tampa Theater.

"Maas Brothers, of course," was the answer when friends asked friends where an item of clothing was available. For many West Coast residents, Maas Brothers was "part of their style," and the Maas Brothers' tradition continues through the words and images in this book.

Though it is altered from its original appearance and its windows are covered and painted, the downtown Tampa store is pictured here standing nobly in the late 1950s. (Courtesy of Sue Meadows.)

One

THE MAAS BROTHERS

The Maas family owned and operated numerous businesses in Georgia. In 1870, Jacob and Sol, the oldest children of Joseph and Fannie Bachrach Maas, opened a small dry-goods business in Cochran, Georgia. Abe, along with his siblings Isaac and Julius, joined his brothers and gained considerable experience at the Cochran store. By the early 1880s, the family split apart. Julius moved to Savannah, and Isaac left for Ocala. Abe loaded up a railcar and set his sights on Tampa, bringing his retailing expertise along with him.

Within a matter of years, Isaac followed Abe to Tampa to aid with his burgeoning department store. Many Maas family members followed and became important business and community leaders, establishing independent clothing stores and retail institutions. The family's merchant legacy was halted on April 29, 1929, when Hahn Department Stores, the forerunner to the Allied Stores Corporation, purchased Abe and Isaac's Tampa department store. After the sale, Abe stepped down as chairman of the board, and Isaac retired as store president. But after the sale, Jerome Waterman, nephew of Abe and Isaac Maas, became the store's new general manager and guided the "Big Store" into decades of growth and prosperity.

ABE MAAS, TAMPA, FLA.

Abe Maas, pioneer merchant of Tampa, was born in Germany, May 28, 1855. He attended the common schools in his native land and, at the age of twenty, came to America.

Mr. Maas went at once to Cochran, Ga., where he joined his brother, Sol Maas, as salesman in a small mercantile business, which he continued for seven years. He then accepted a position as a traveling salesman and was on the road for two years, traveling out of Macon, Ga. Until 1886 he conducted stores in Dublin and Cochran, Ga., and then decided to move to Florida.

The present big business of Maas Bros. dates from Abe Maas's arrival in Tampa in 1886. He started the store alone but was soon joined by his brother, Isaac, in 1887, and the house became Maas Brothers, at the corner of Twiggs and Franklin streets, then known as the Field Building, 23x90 feet.

The establishment was a very limited one at first, but it grew as the town grew, and in 1898 they moved to the present store, occupying two floors 50x90, and, at present, it is the largest of its kind in the State. From one small store room it expanded into a department store, occupying three floors of an entire building at Franklin and Zack streets. Even these quarters have proved insufficient, and the firm has bought the American National Bank Building, across the street from the old store, and is also building a modern eight-story building at Tampa and Zack streets, adjoining the former American Bank Building, four floors of which will also be occupied by the Maas department store.

Mr. Maas has always been active in public affairs in Tampa and is recognized as one of the most valuable citizens in movements for the advancement of the city. He has been a member of the Tampa Board of Trade since 1886, and a director of that organization for all of that period, with the exception of one year. He has been one of the powers for good in the Board and his effective work has counted in practically every movement that has been undertaken in the interest of Tampa.

Born on May 28, 1855, in Dolgesheim, Germany, Abe Maas immigrated to America in 1870 and joined his brothers at the family business in Cochran, Georgia. After the death of his father and the demise of the Cochran business, Abe relocated to Tampa in November 1886. He filled a boxcar train full of merchandise and opened his first store at Franklin and Twiggs Streets. Abe Maas led the business through numerous expansions. In 1931, Abe reported that the company's success was based on "the best goods of standard make at lowest prices to our customers, backed by our guarantee of satisfactory service." Up until his death in 1941, Abe served as the company's chairman of the board. He was regarded as "one of the city's most valuable citizens" and was active as the Tampa Board of Trade's director for many years. According to niece Aubrey Maas Shine, Abe was "a big man" who was "always very sweet and nice." (Courtesy of the University of South Florida Library.)

ISAAC MAAS, TAMPA, FLA.

Isaac Maas, merchant, one of the leading business men of Tampa, was born in Germany, October 14, 1851. After attending the common schools in his native country, he came to the United States in 1877.

Joining in the general movement toward the South, regarded as the land of opportunity, young Maas settled at Cochran, Ga., engaging in the dry goods business, which was to be his life work. He spent a year at Savannah, Ga., and conducted a business for two years at Ocala, Fla.

Attracted by the promise of Tampa, Mr. Maas moved to that city in 1887, and, with his brother, Abe Maas, established the house of Maas Brothers, which has grown into the largest department store in South Florida.

Maas Brothers began in a small store room, with a very limited stock. The business acumen and untiring energy of Isaac Maas was mainly instrumental in the growth of the business from 1,100 feet of floor space to 26,000 feet; from a sales force of three to more than 100; from a capital of $625 to $250,000; from one of the smallest to the largest exclusive ladies furnishing goods houses in the State.

The growth of the business is evidently just beginning, for the firm is now having built a new and modern building, at Tampa and Zack streets, adjoining the building formerly owned by the American National Bank, the two buildings together to comprise the new home of the company and to constitute what will be the largest department store in Florida. Every modern idea is being incorporated in the new store and it will be one of the prides and one of the show places of Tampa.

Isaac Maas is the secretary and general manager of Maas Bros., which company now includes besides the original founders, Isaac and Abe Maas, Ernest and Sol Maas, J. A. Waterman and C. A. McKay. He is also a vice-president of the Citizens-American Bank and Trust Company and interested and closely identified with other leading Tampa concerns.

Mr. Maas is a Shriner, a Mason, an Elk, a Rotarian, a member of the Tampa Yacht and Country Club, of the two local golf clubs and other organizations. During the World War, he took a very active part in conducting Liberty Loan and other war work campaigns. He is intensely patriotic and progressive and never fails to respond to a call for work or financial assistance to a good cause.

Mr. Maas is unmarried. He has traveled extensively and has made several tours of Europe. He is a patron of fine arts and owns a valuable private collection of paintings and statuary.

Isaac Maas was born on October 14, 1851, and arrived in Cochran, Georgia, in 1877. After the family business dissolved, Isaac operated a dry-goods store in Savannah before he relocated to Ocala, Florida, another growing Florida city. Isaac grew frustrated with Ocala and joined his brother in Tampa in 1887. Like his brother Abe, he was active in community affairs. Isaac Maas was a Shriner, a Mason, an Elk, a Rotarian, and a vice president of the Citizens-American bank. He was described as a "patron of fine arts" and owned numerous valuable paintings and statuary. Isaac was "gruff," says Aubrey Maas Shine, and "the two brothers were very different and acted as if they didn't come from the same family." However, only a few months after Isaac arrived in Tampa, the two men left the city due to a yellow fever epidemic. Isaac never had children and passed away in 1935. (Courtesy of the University of South Florida Library.)

The original Tampa store was named the Palace Dry Goods. At the time, there were only about a dozen businesses that operated in the city's core business area. Abe and his wife, Bena, were always on hand and greeted customers. The one-room storefront always stayed open until the last customer left the store, which could be as late as midnight. The Palace Dry Goods was the first Florida business to adopt a one-price policy. Abe Maas once stated, "We have just one price to everybody. We sell merchandise as cheaply as possible but treat everyone the same." In April 1887, one of Tampa's earliest streetlights was installed outside of the Palace store. (Courtesy of the University of South Florida Library.)

When the yellow fever epidemic subsided in January 1888, the Maas brothers returned to Tampa and stocked the store with fresh merchandise. The two men made frequent buying trips to New York and returned to their eagerly waiting customers. Members of the Maas family, including Abe Maas on the far right, pose for a photograph outside the reopened business. (Courtesy of the University of South Florida Library.)

The company, renamed Maas Brothers in November 1888, moved from its original location to a new, bigger structure at Franklin and Zach Streets in 1898. Now located in the Krause Building, the brothers expanded the store and kept up with Tampa's growing population. (Courtesy of the University of South Florida Library.)

With the advent of the automobile, Maas Brothers initiated Tampa's earliest delivery service. By the early part of the 20th century, Maas Brothers was delivering carpets, draperies, and awnings to its customers. (Courtesy of the Tampa–Hillsborough County Public Library.)

After working and gaining experience in his brothers' Tampa business, Julius Maas, the youngest Maas sibling, opened Maas the Haberdasher on Franklin Street. Julius arrived in Tampa in 1893 and opened his own store in 1901. Maas the Haberdasher became one of the largest clothing businesses in the city. (Courtesy of the Tampa–Hillsborough County Public Library.)

Julius Maas relocated his haberdashery into the Krause Building after Abe and Isaac vacated the storefront for their new department store. Julius Maas was joined by his nephew Julius Weil, and the store was renamed Weil-Maas. Cousin Ernest Maas operated his own ladies' store from 1929 to 1937 and later joined Weil-Maas. Weil-Maas was destroyed by fire on June 20, 1951, and never reopened. Members of Ernest Maas's family currently operate Kirbys on Dale Mabry Highway. (Courtesy of the Tampa–Hillsborough County Public Library.)

This 1911 view of Franklin Street looking north from Zach Street features an advertisement for the Tampa Electric Co. that reads "For a Brighter Tampa." Before he joined the Maas Brothers store as a stock boy, Abe's son, Sol, worked for Tampa Electric. (Courtesy of the Tampa–Hillsborough County Public Library.)

Arguably, the most influential Maas family member during modern times was Jerome Waterman. Waterman joined the company in 1907 at age 23. He worked his way up from bookkeeper to advertising manager to president and chairman of the board. Waterman assembled a powerful management team that expanded the business beyond its Tampa headquarters. He had a magnetic personality and was a community figurehead. Over the course of his tenure, Jerome Waterman helped grow the business from $1.6 million in annual sales to over $85 million in 1968. Waterman passed away in 1970 at age 86. Vice president of credit Robert Walton remembers Jerome Waterman as "a big teddy bear." Walton says that Waterman would occasionally ask Walton to "go easy" on some of Jerome's friends during harder times. This photograph shows Jerome Waterman hosting a fashion show in 1947. (Courtesy of the Tampa–Hillsborough County Public Library.)

Two

BUILDING A TRADITION

By the early 1900s, many successful dry-goods stores evolved into powerful modern department stores. These emporiums carried everything for everybody, and most of these businesses introduced unique merchandise, from ready-to-wear clothing to washing machines, to their loyal customers. Shoppers relied on department stores for their merchandise, services, and traditions.

In Tampa, Maas Brothers was *the* department store. In 1921, the company opened a new $500,000 complex that was billed as Florida's second-largest department store. The *Tampa Tribune* praised the new store for "giving Tampa, and south Florida patrons the best possible service and the most attractive and desirable merchandise." Its "Aisles of Beauty" and unique home fashions, along with its Colonial Tea Room and Fountainette earned Maas Brothers the title of "Florida West Coast's One Stop Shopping Center."

On April 27, 1929, Maas Brothers was purchased by retail holding company Hahn Department Stores. Abe and Isaac Maas retired from the business, and Hahn assumed overall control. Hahn provided a central executive headquarters that left the managing and buying decisions in local hands. Hahn stumbled during the Depression years and reorganized into the Allied Stores Corporation in 1935. For many years, Maas Brothers was one of Allied's most profitable divisions. Allied frequently invested in Maas Brothers, and the downtown Tampa store developed into a statewide shopping destination. With Allied's executive support and financial backing, Maas Brothers brought the most modern retailing techniques and services to Tampa.

Audrey Maas Shine, the niece of Abe and Isaac Maas, recalls the Tampa store as a "warm and personal place." Shine continues, "When you mentioned the term 'department store,' you knew that Maas Brothers was the store to go. It's always the case when I say hello and people hear my name 'Maas,' they *always* say that they sure miss Maas Brothers."

On February 7, 1907, Maas Brothers was incorporated. Abe Maas was named company president, and his brother Isaac became secretary/treasurer. The company mission statement read, "The reputation of this establishment is based on the quality of the goods we sell, the excellent values offered and a highly satisfactory store service." In order to keep up with the city's growth, Maas Brothers sought larger quarters. In July 1917, the company began work on the Citrus Exchange Building. The eight-story building, constructed with reinforced concrete, was built to house the department store on its first four floors, with offices, including the Florida Citrus Exchange, on its upper floors. Every piece of material used was made in Tampa. The Citrus Exchange was completed in May 1920, but Maas Brothers did not occupy the building until the following year. (Courtesy of the Tampa–Hillsborough County Public Library.)

Maas Brothers' Citrus Exchange Building was on the southeast corner of Tampa and Zach Streets. It gave Maas Brothers the distinction of being Florida's second-largest department store. The cost of the new structure was in excess of $1 million. It was billed as "one of the greatest building achievements ever accomplished in Florida." During the building's construction, the neighboring American National Bank became available on Franklin Street. Maas Brothers reconfigured the bank into a department store and connected it to the new Citrus Exchange. Other neighboring buildings, including the former Strand Theatre, were incorporated into the Maas Brothers complex. After the Citrus Exchange moved out in 1938, the Tampa Avenue structure was officially renamed the Maas Brothers Building. (Courtesy of the Tampa–Hillsborough County Public Library.)

On October 18, 1921, the new Maas Brothers department store, the city's largest business, celebrated its official grand opening. The four-story department store afforded citizens every modern convenience found at stores in other large American cities. The former one-room store now contained over 70,000 square feet of selling space. (Courtesy of the Tampa–Hillsborough County Public Library.)

Within a few years after its 1921 grand opening, Maas Brothers added another two floors to its Franklin Street building. The company billed itself as "Florida West Coast's One Stop Shopping Center." This photograph from 1946 shows the two added floors, as well as other businesses, along the 600 block of Franklin Street. (Courtesy of the Tampa–Hillsborough County Public Library.)

In most American cities, department stores played crucial roles during the holidays. Large stores offered elaborate displays along with unique and exclusive merchandise. In 1931, Maas Brothers decorated its entire Franklin Street frontage for Christmas. (Courtesy of the Tampa–Hillsborough County Public Library.)

Large department stores offered unique services to their customers and employees. Many employee benefits, including an executive-training program, were offered at Maas Brothers. One early benefit to employees and customers was an in-store lending library. This library offered an educational service and instilled repeat visits by customers. (Courtesy of the University of South Florida Library.)

LENDING LIBRARY

ROMANTIC LOVE STORIES
MYSTERIES

POPULAR FICTION
NON-FICTION

Maas Brothers of Tampa

Central Florida's One Stop Shopping Center

Maas Brothers

The downtown Tampa Maas Brothers store was nearing its height of popularity during the late 1930s. Tampa was the center of commerce in the region, and its economic and political power towered over other area localities. This photograph shows the Maas Brothers store, along with many overhead electrical streetcar wires, in 1939. (Courtesy of the Tampa–Hillsborough County Public Library.)

In the early 1940s, the Tampa Maas Brothers added more streamlined exterior features that included a vertical electric sign. The white building at the neighboring Franklin Street corner shows the renovated Maas the Haberdasher business. Ernest Maas's ladies' wear store is located to the left of the haberdashery. (Courtesy of the University of South Florida Library.)

Sales clerks and shoppers fill the downtown store's main floor in 1929. The departments shown include costume jewelry, handkerchiefs, greeting cards, and hosiery sales and repair. The mezzanine level can be seen at upper left. (Courtesy of the Tampa–Hillsborough County Public Library.)

This photograph from 1928 shows a relatively quiet sales floor. Traditional bolts of fabric are sold alongside hosiery, neckwear, and laces. (Courtesy of the Tampa–Hillsborough County Public Library.)

Pictured here in 1929 is the designer-shoe salon. The department did not offer any self-service options, and no special sales or offerings are advertised. Stacks of shoeboxes can be seen on the right. (Courtesy of the Tampa–Hillsborough County Public Library.)

One of the most important departments that large stores offered was millinery. Hats were not only specially fitted but also trimmed, or decorated, according to the customers' wishes. Maas Brothers prominently advertised "Campus Hats by Lazarus." This millinery department image dates from 1929. (Courtesy of the Tampa–Hillsborough County Public Library.)

The busy intersection of Franklin and Zach Streets is pictured here in 1934. The display windows that encircle the first floor of the Maas Brothers store are part of the largest plate-glass windows in the state of Florida. (Courtesy of the Tampa–Hillsborough County Public Library.)

Shoppers crowd the main floor of Maas Brothers during 1946. Customers are taking advantage of the store's popular end-of-month clearance sale. In the photograph, shoppers can chose from 50¢ toilet water, 39¢ place mats, and handbags from $2 to $3. (Courtesy of the Tampa–Hillsborough County Public Library.)

Department stores often offered dining facilities for their customers as a service. They provided solid good food and encouraged shoppers to stay inside the store and not leave its doors. Maas Brothers' Tampa store housed two restaurants: the formal Neptune Room and the casual Fountainette lunch counter. The Neptune Room was formerly called the Colonial Tea Room and was located on the store's second floor. The Fountainette was on the store's first floor and balcony. It served breakfast, luncheon, and afternoon tea. This Fountainette menu dates from July 12, 1943.

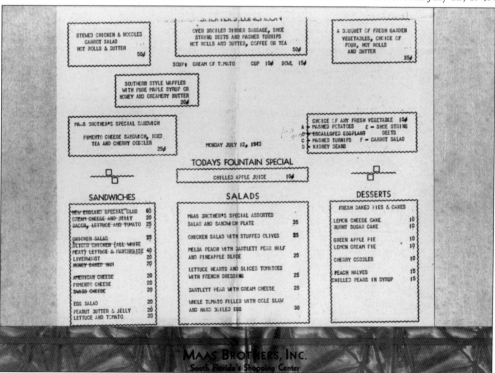

This photograph of the glass-brick Fountainette lunch counter dates from 1946. Located just opposite of the department store's haberdashery, numerous pineapples and citrus fruits line the luncheonette's soda bar. (Courtesy of the Tampa–Hillsborough County Public Library.)

Maas Brothers' formal Colonial Tea Room restaurant was the site of numerous fashion shows and hosted parties, card clubs, and meetings. In 1946, the Colonial Tea Room included a cigar counter that featured Hav-A-Tampa and Admiration brand products for its patrons. (Courtesy of the Tampa–Hillsborough County Public Library.)

Maas Brothers celebrated its 50th anniversary in 1936. The department store's golden-jubilee year featured the slogan "Forward March." One advertisement from the celebration stated, "Our hearts palpitate with pride when we look back upon the growth and development of fifty years of progress. Just 50 years ago, Abe Maas started a small enterprise which is now represented by this modern establishment . . . Dedicated to our customers and employees who have made this '50 years of service a reality,' to them and to all South Florida, we say Happy New Year." This photograph from April 16, 1936, features the attendees of the store's 50th-anniversary banquet. Former director of training and development Joanne Timmer Zabaldo reflects on her time as a store executive: "Maas Brothers was a very special place and fostered a very special, large family of employees and customers. We were a great training ground, with Presidents of Gimbels, Marshall Field's and many Allied stores all having started at Maas Bros. And those who shared their talent elsewhere would agree with us who stayed—the culture of Maas Brothers was, and is still, unique in the industry." (Courtesy of the Tampa–Hillsborough County Public Library.)

Pictured here are the main floor and mezzanine of the downtown Tampa store. Maas Brothers was celebrating its 60th year of business. In 1946, the first-floor merchandise included cosmetics, jewelry, notions, handbags, stationery, handkerchiefs, and the men's sport shop. (Courtesy of the Tampa–Hillsborough County Public Library.)

In 1929, Maas Brothers was home to Tampa's largest selection of toys. Dolls, stuffed animals, wagons, books, and erector sets were among the goods for sale. In its earlier years, the building's windows allowed light to shine on the sales floor. The marquee for the Tampa Theater can be seen outside the toy department's windows. (Courtesy of the Tampa–Hillsborough County Public Library.)

Maas Brothers' Junior World department is pictured here in 1946. The store carried the then-popular line of Carlye junior dresses, the predecessor to the Leslie Fay clothing line. The mannequin advertised "Maas Brothers Easter Basket of Color."

Back in 1946, the main-floor merchandise included clocks, silverware, gloves, and the store's beauty shop. Exclusive Dorothy Gray cold cream and lipstick, Max Factor and Revlon cosmetics, Hansen gloves, and Mimosa Bouquet perfumes were some of the goods available at Maas Brothers. (Courtesy of the Tampa–Hillsborough County Public Library.)

From its earliest years, Maas Brothers always carried an extensive line of home merchandise and furnishings. In this 1946 photograph, figurines and decorative cans are interspersed in the store's lamp department. The store also carried a large collection of the Roseville pottery line. (Courtesy of the Tampa–Hillsborough County Public Library.)

Trifari costume jewelry was sold alongside elaborate greeting cards and specialty handbags. Maas Brothers Easter Basket of Color, a 1946 sales promotion, was promoted on its sales counters and merchandise signage. Greeting cards were priced between 50¢ and $2.49. (Courtesy of the Tampa–Hillsborough County Public Library.)

No other department was more important during Maas Brothers' 1946 Easter Basket of Color promotion than the millinery section. The featured item was "The Easter Bonnet—Beloved by all." Brands featured included Milgrim, Brewster, Evelyn Varon, Diana, Valerie, and Dobbs. (Courtesy of the Tampa–Hillsborough County Public Library.)

In earlier years, many American department stores carried extensive grocery selections. Grocery stores such as Publix, Kwik Chek, and A&P did not develop a self-service format until the 1940s and 1950s. In the mid-1940s, Maas Brothers grocery selection offered canned produce and meat, imported cheese, frozen meat, seafood, and vegetables, and a large assortment of jams and marmalades. (Courtesy of the Tampa–Hillsborough County Public Library.)

In the 1940s, Tampa's Franklin Street was almost exclusively the holiday shopping and entertainment destination for the region. This photograph shows the elaborate decorations that crossed the street, along with signage for the Tampa Theater. (Courtesy of the Tampa–Hillsborough County Public Library.)

Holiday shopping was in full swing when this photograph was taken on Friday afternoon, December 6, 1946. Crowds of shoppers dwarf Christmas wreaths and large Santa Clauses. A war-bond sales counter, a typical offering for a department store, was located on the main floor. (Courtesy of the Tampa–Hillsborough County Public Library.)

By the mid-1940s, Tampa was the economic and social epicenter of the Tampa Bay area. Maas Brothers had a thriving operation on one of the city's main downtown corners. Melvin Stein, a former Maas Brothers president, reflected on the company's position after the end of the war. In 1968, Stein wrote, "Up to the year 1948, the people living along the entire West Coast of Florida, who wished to shop at Maas Brothers, which was the dominant and largest quality department store in the area, had to take the sometimes long trip to this one store in Tampa to take care of needs and desires. To insure keeping up with the growth of Florida and to make the most of present and future opportunities, it was time to make changes in the way people shopped. The stores should be located conveniently and nearby to the places where people lived and where they could get to easily, instead of having to travel great distances and to other cities." (Courtesy of the Tampa–Hillsborough County Public Library.)

Three

BEACH BOUND

On February 24, 1945, store president Jerome A. Waterman announced plans for a second Maas Brothers store. The company chose downtown St. Petersburg, over 20 miles from its Tampa headquarters, for its next location. The new ultra-modern St. Petersburg store was the result of almost three years of planning. Waterman stated, "Our aim is and has been to establish one of the finest department stores in the state in St. Petersburg. We want this to be as much a St. Petersburg development as possible." The company chose the intersection of First Avenue North and Third Street, the Sunshine Corner, for its new store.

Maas Brothers fully opened its new St. Petersburg location on February 10, 1948, almost three years after the initial announcement. Its modernistic décor was in sharp contrast to its older Tampa counterpart. Its broad main floor, along with a mezzanine balcony, was highlighted by a succession of windows that wrapped around the store. With its multitude of services and merchandise offerings, the new store changed the way St. Petersburg shopped.

"We really had a business going there," says credit manager Robert Walton. "We had all these things going for us in St. Petersburg. It was the top performing store and a real friendly operation." Director of stores Talbot Boudreau echoes, "The St. Petersburg store was fantastic. It was such a class act. Very profitable and very prominent in the area."

In 1961, Maas Brothers expanded its St. Petersburg store. It developed into a part of St. Petersburg's identity, and its Sunshine Tea Room was a community landmark. In its heyday, over 700 employees helped sell designer fashions alongside refrigerators, fabric, records, paint, and guns. Its talking Christmas tree, Nativity-scene window, and semiannual Blockbuster Sales were local traditions.

When Maas Brothers announced its new St. Petersburg store in February 1945, the company envisioned a five-story building at the southeast corner of Fourth Street and First Avenue North. Four floors were devoted to air-conditioned shopping while the top floor was planned to feature a glassed-in tea room. The Penn-Flora Hotel occupied the planned site of the department store. However, the company decided that the hotel site was insufficient in size and chose the northeast corner of First Avenue and Third Street North for its new store. Company president Jerome Waterman made this announcement on December 2, 1945. Maas Brothers also acquired the Harrison Furniture and Hardware building on Central Avenue. Waterman called the St. Petersburg Maas Brothers "the last word in modern store development." It was the first store that the Allied Stores Corporation, Maas Brothers' corporate parent, built from the ground up. (Courtesy of the Tampa–Hillsborough County Public Library.)

As a result of the purchase of Harrison's, Maas Brothers incorporated the landmark St. Petersburg home-furnishings store into the lower floor of its new department store. The new Harrison Galleries at Maas Brothers sold home furnishings along with housewares. The Harrison Galleries opened on January 12, 1948, almost a month before the rest of the department store.

Harrison Galleries

OPENS   TOMORROW

A beautiful new setting for an old St. Petersburg institution . . . an entire floor of your shining new department store

MAAS
ST. PETERSBURG
Brothers

Who's Polly?
That's Me!...

Polly Sunshine

Your Guiding Light To Better Buys At MAAS Brothers
BUDGET CORNER.... OPENS TODAY 9:30 A. M.

TEMPORARY LOCATION First Avenue North at Fourth Street
STORE HOURS 9:30 A. M. TO 5:45 P. M. DAILY

MAAS
ST. PETERSBURG
Brothers
BUDGET

On January 12, 1948, Polly Sunshine unlocked the doors of a temporary budget shop on the site of the former Harrison's store. Polly Sunshine's name was chosen after the department store called its new location the Sunshine Corner, as sunshine was the city's "most famous commodity." The budget shop eventually moved to the second floor of Maas Brothers.

Maas Brothers officially opened its St. Petersburg store on February 10, 1948. Though Tampa was still the headquarters operation and employed over 800 people, this new branch employed 200 St. Petersburg people. It was larger than the Tampa store and offered a multitude of services: the Sunshine Tearoom and Fountainette, a bridal shop, beauty salon, lending library, photo studio, bake shop, delicatessen, Jane Lee tele-shopping, home delivery, interior decorating, and watch, jewelry, shoe, hosiery, and fur repair, among others. The store was an immediate success, and store president Jerome Waterman outlined the reasons behind its popularity. Waterman felt that a good store must be in a good location, and the business must have vision and courage. He also believed in giving employees the ability to exercise judgment and make decisions. Civic development and involvement was also a crucial element of Waterman's business plan.

The sleek and modern St. Petersburg Maas Brothers store gave a commanding presence to the city's downtown, especially at night. Its usage of stylized signage and lighting clearly set it apart from the Tampa headquarters store. A 55-foot-tall pylon that spelled Maas revolved every 60 seconds. The St. Petersburg store was rarely advertised along with the Tampa store and gave the impression that it operated as a separate entity. (Courtesy of the St. Petersburg Museum of History.)

The St. Petersburg store was a popular shopping destination for the Sunshine City and brought many new shopping conveniences to the area. This photograph provides a panoramic view of the first floor during a Maas Days promotion. It also shows the sweeping mezzanine that housed the Sunshine Room restaurant and Men's Grill. (Courtesy of the Tampa–Hillsborough County Public Library.)

Christmas shoppers flocked to the St. Petersburg store, just as generations of customers did at the Tampa location. The St. Petersburg Maas Brothers featured modern escalators, Santa Claus visits, and an extensive fruit-shipping counter.

Well-dressed customers shop the large men's department, which received sunlight from large glass windows. The store carried a large selection of business suits and sport coats. A small camera department was located alongside the escalator bank. (Courtesy of the St. Petersburg Museum of History.)

The St. Petersburg store was well known for its popular 234-seat Sunshine Room restaurant. The mezzanine restaurant afforded diners a panoramic view of the busy main floor. The Sunshine Room offered "air-conditioning, really comfortable chairs, and fine murals," according to company documents. The restaurant served lunch, tea from 2:00 to 4:00 p.m., and dinner until 7:00 p.m. The first-floor Fountainette lunch counter sat 139 diners. (Courtesy of the St. Petersburg Museum of History.)

The St. Petersburg store was designed by Tampa architect Leo Elliott. The store carried a large merchandise selection that rivaled Tampa but utilized modern retailing techniques. This photograph, taken shortly after the store's grand opening, features the large china department. (Courtesy of the St. Petersburg Museum of History.)

The St. Petersburg store celebrated its 69th-anniversary sale in 1955 in combination with the city's annual Festival of States. Crowds shopped the store's main floor, which was decorated with state flags hung over bargains such as 69¢ handbags, $1.99 blouses, and $3.97 housedresses. (Both, courtesy of the St. Petersburg Museum of History.)

Maas Brothers' St. Petersburg store earned the distinction of being Florida's first completely air-conditioned department store. This air-conditioning unit was billed as the largest single unit in the South. Downtown department stores formerly relied on windows to cool their selling floors. By the 1960s, most of these older businesses were at least partially air-conditioned. Store advertisements told customers to "Shop in Cooled Comfort."

In May 1960, Maas Brothers disclosed plans that expanded the St. Petersburg store by 50 percent. The company planned two new structures, one for fashions and the other for home furnishings, attached to the existing building. Manager Alfred L. Schelm proclaimed that the additions would "make Maas Brothers St. Petersburg one of the largest stores in the state and one of the most beautiful in the country." However, when the new addition expanded into the original building, the workers found that the floors were eight inches off. The architects spent time smoothing out the connection. (Courtesy of the St. Petersburg Museum of History.)

Al Schelm (right) stands next to attorney William Allison in February 1960. Allison's family operated the former Allison Hotel, which was redeveloped as the store's new parking facility. Schelm "was a great leader," states Ron Rodriguez. "He told us that since we were in the fashion business, we had to wear long sleeve white shirts. He also taught us how to tie our ties! He was just that way."

Display windows were just as important in St. Petersburg as they were in downtown Tampa. These unique windows were originally designed to combine fluorescent and incandescent lighting. They continually wrapped the exterior at the store's main corner. The louvered ceilings were utilized so that the observer would not see light bulbs. (Courtesy of the St. Petersburg Museum of History.)

Four

SUNCOASTING

After its initial branch store success in St. Petersburg, Maas Brothers entered a period of growth. It targeted downtown shopping areas along Florida's West Coast and eventually spread into new suburban shopping centers. The downtown Tampa store remained the corporate headquarters, but its retail popularity diminished. As the company expanded, its offices required more space, and large selling areas of the store were transitioned for that purpose. Like other American downtowns, Tampa experienced white flight and competed with the enticements of suburban living and free parking. But Maas Brothers knew that there was life beyond downtown Tampa, and its new suburban stores kept up with the area's growing population.

In 1954, Maas Brothers chose downtown Lakeland for its third store, followed by downtown Sarasota in 1958 and downtown Clearwater in 1961. A separate Store for Homes opened on Gandy Boulevard in 1956. In 1966, Maas Brothers at West Shore Plaza introduced the Tampa Bay area to large-scale suburban shopping. Located only five miles from the city's core, Maas Brothers' West Shore Plaza store quickly surpassed its downtown location as the company's new flagship. Through the 1970s, suburban growth continued throughout West Florida, from Tallahassee to Naples.

As it expanded into new markets, Maas Brothers believed its success would be based on credit card saturation. "Gainesville had a population of 25,000 but 10,000 were college students. We had to weed out the students," said credit manager Robert Walton. "Lakeland was not a densely populated area and the customers were scattered. Sarasota was more concise. Ft. Myers was a good store but Naples was a very influential store. Its average area income was very high and we had some very successful special credit card events. We actively promoted our slogan, 'A Maas Brothers credit card . . . It's better than money.' "

Ron Rodriguez, former vice president of special events, proudly stated, "Maas Brothers was a wonderful part of my professional career and my life. I am very proud of Maas Brothers, what we did, how we did it, and the contributions we made to the cities where we were located." Vice president of stores Talbot Boudreau commented, "Do you see all of those beautiful storefronts in the shopping centers today? I built them!"

Maas Brothers initiated an executive-training program in the 1960s. According to notes by former president Melvin Stein, the program provided "an opportunity for ambitious and qualified salespeople and low level employees to move up to supervisory and management level positions in the company. This gave many local people [the ability] to find desirable career opportunities right here where they lived. [Many] people who were salespeople, clericals, and stock people have risen to high level executive and management positions within Maas Brothers and other companies within the Allied Stores organization." Maas Brothers enjoyed strong leadership over the years. This photograph shows the store's 1954 management team. From left to right are K.D. Rippey (secretary and controller), Ray Hough (general sales manager), Al Schelm (vice president), Jerome Waterman, Melvin Stein (executive vice president and managing director), Henri Guertin (merchandise vice president for all fashion departments), and Lee Graham (merchandise vice president for all home furnishings). Not shown are John W. Schaub Sr. (vice president), William P. Key (assistant secretary) and John W. Schaub Jr. (St. Petersburg operation manager). (Courtesy of Richard N. Stein)

Melvin S. Stein became president and managing director of Maas Brothers in 1958. He was named executive vice president and managing director in 1954 when Jerome Waterman retired. Waterman was permitted to retain the title of president and an office at that time as a courtesy since he was a nephew of the original Maas brothers. Stein retired in 1970 at the age of 65, due to Allied's mandatory-retirement rules. He was actively involved and took a leadership position in a number of local biracial- and human-relations committees composed of prominent white and black leaders. Robert Walton said Mel Stein "was Maas Brothers. He was a gentleman and a merchant." (Courtesy of Richard N. Stein)

Directors of the Allied Stores Corporation gather at the Gandy Store for Homes sometime in the late 1950s. (Courtesy of Richard N. Stein.)

On November 1, 1954, Maas Brothers opened a store in downtown Lakeland. Located on the city's Imperial Corner at Kentucky and Lemon Streets, the Lakeland Maas Brothers was Polk County's only complete department store. The company celebrated the Lakeland grand opening by combining it with Jubilee Month. The Lakeland store was geared toward loyal Maas Brothers customers who grew tired of making the 35-mile trip to downtown Tampa. But the company underestimated the store's popularity. It was too small for its high volume of business and Maas Brothers rebuilt the store in 1970. After its grand opening, Maas Brothers frequently advertised the Lakeland store in its Tampa newspaper promotions and not its St. Petersburg location. Above is a rare view of the rear of the original Lakeland store during an early Christmas season.

The original Maas Brothers warehouse was located in Tampa at Thirteenth and Twiggs Streets. The property was one of several, including the downtown Tampa store, that the family sold to the Maas Realty Company. This independent realty company was formed shortly before the department store was sold in 1929. By the mid-1950s, Maas Brothers needed an updated warehouse for its growing business. According to notes by former president Melvin Stein, the company's success was based on further expansion. "Studies were started, programs developed, objectives set, and plans made for the gradual expansion of new stores through the entire trading area. This involved projecting where the population growth would be, checking the major existing and planned highways and the likely new areas for major residential development and establishing possible locations for building stores and shopping malls." In order to update its facilities and better serve the housing development, Maas Brothers designed a new Store for Homes and a service building on Gandy Boulevard. (Courtesy of the Tampa–Hillsborough County Public Library.)

Maas Brothers opened its "magnificent Store for Homes for today's living" on January 30, 1956. Located on Gandy Boulevard between Dale Mabry Highway and Manhattan Avenue, the Store for Homes was billed as the South's largest and finest home-furnishings store. Maas Brothers chose the site because of its convenience to residents of both Tampa and St. Petersburg along with its ability to offer ample free parking. The Store for Homes included a bridal consultant service, fur-storage vaults, and gifts for the home. Maas Brothers stated that its new Store for Homes "will not only roll out the red carpet to the people of Central Florida, but that carpet will be the best in nylon." (Both, courtesy of the Tampa–Hillsborough County Public Library.)

The new service building was located immediately behind the Gandy Store for Homes. The massive structure continually expanded over the years and grew to over 700,000 square feet by the 1970s. Workers often traveled by bicycles throughout the facility because of its size. The service building always utilized state-of-the-art technology as it processed the merchandise. (Courtesy of the St. Petersburg Museum of History.)

In November 1956, Maas Brothers opened an apparel store at the Northgate Shopping Center. Originally designed as a children's shop, the 17,000-square-foot store remained in business until January 1982. (Courtesy of the St. Petersburg Museum of History.)

In February 1955, Pres. Jerome Waterman announced plans for a downtown Sarasota store. At the press conference, Waterman said, "For some years, we have been looking to Sarasota, Bradenton, and the area adjacent to these thriving cities with the idea of bringing a modern, up-to-date department store to that section of Florida. This is because we realized the rapid growth which this part of Florida is enjoying now and will continue to enjoy." Patterned after the St. Petersburg store, Maas Brothers opened its "truly amazing, luxurious, tremendous" Sarasota location on October 1, 1956. Sarasota's first mayor and one of its oldest natives, A.B. Edwards, cut the ribbon to the store. Edwards praised the accomplishments of the company founders. "May we cherish these names [Abe and Isaac] in our time as theirs is no more." The store was located at Washington Boulevard and Main Street.

MAAS BROTHERS

TAMPA 1886

ST. PETERSBURG 1948

LAKELAND 1954

GANDY 1956

SARASOTA 1956

CLEARWATER 195?

This collage shows all of the company stores that operated in the 1950s, with the exception of the Northgate apparel store. It lists Clearwater as a planned location. Former executive vice president Chuck James recalls the excitement behind the store's continuous expansions. "It was obvious that Maas Brothers had a huge opportunity to quickly expand up and down the West Coast of Florida. We had the full financial backing of our parent company, Allied Stores, to go for it! Over a relatively short time we opened stores from Naples on the south to Gainesville on the north and every major market in between. I was fortunate to be in the right place at the right time regarding my career with Maas Brothers, as I became an employee who participated with all the expansion along the way." (Courtesy of the University of South Florida Library.)

The Clearwater Maas Brothers opened on October 23, 1961. Located on a prime piece of waterfront property, the store's opening was timed with the company's 75th anniversary. Located in the heart of downtown, "this fine store will satisfy your every need; shopping trips to other cities will no longer be necessary." Home to the popular Suncoast Room restaurant, the Clearwater branch greatly expanded in size four years later. These photographs were taken shortly after the store's opening in 1961. (Both, courtesy of the Tampa–Hillsborough County Public Library.)

In the fall of 1965, Maas Brothers opened its first complete shopping center department store. Located at the Edison Mall in Fort Myers, Maas Brothers' investment was indicative of the area's growth and potential. This image shows the mall entrance. The store's opening featured a live organ performance by Kephart for Music stores. (Courtesy of the St. Petersburg Museum of History.)

Maas Brothers' Gandy Boulevard Store for Homes maintained its popularity and relevance for many years. In addition to furniture, the store also featured an outdoor shop. Customers could purchase everything from boats and golf equipment to jalousie windows and awnings.

By 1966, Maas Brothers wanted to improve and strengthen its position in Tampa. The company spent considerable time and resources outside of its hometown, and felt that it was time to rebuild its image at home. In an advertisement in the *Tampa Tribune*, Maas Brothers stated, "Since our beginning, in 1886, we have offered tangible evidence to support our belief that Tampa is destined to be one of Florida's great cities. By expanding, diversifying and maintaining a tradition of integrity, quality, and good taste, we have endeavored to serve Tampa and Tampans. In recent years, the opening of our beautiful Gandy Boulevard Store for Homes, the Maas Casual Shop at North Gate and the remodeling of our downtown store are further examples of our faith in the future." The business now focused on suburban sites in shopping malls, and the perfect location was at Tampa's new West Shore Plaza.

Maas Brothers' West Shore Plaza store opened almost a year before the rest of the area's first enclosed shopping mall. It had an extremely prominent location from the highway and near the airport. Its popular Suncoast Room restaurant offered an expansive view from its prominent glass windows. With ample parking and late hours, it quickly became the area's premiere destination department store. (Courtesy of the University of South Florida Library.)

Opened on October 28, 1966, Maas Brothers' West Shore Plaza store, according to president Melvin Stein, "resulted in West Shore becoming the major concentrated location of office buildings, hotels, banks, retail stores, and related activities." (Courtesy of the University of South Florida Library.)

After its successful West Shore opening, Maas Brothers expanded to the Gainesville Mall. Opened in February 1968, the Gainesville Mall location was the final store that opened under president Melvin Stein's tenure. Stein retired in 1970. That same year, chairman Jerome Waterman, Abe Maas's nephew, suddenly passed away. This ushered in a new era of company leadership.

In July 1968, Maas Brothers made a decision to rebuild its undersized downtown Lakeland store in favor of a total renovation and expansion of the existing structure. Not long after the original Lakeland store opened in 1954, the company realized it made a mistake regarding its small size. Polk County "indicated a tremendous growth potential for the next two or three decades," according to company documents. Maas Brothers opted to build the new store in the former store's parking lot, at Kentucky and Orange Streets. The older location remained in operation until the new store was completed. The City of Lakeland assisted the store with parking needs and incentives in order to keep Maas Brothers downtown. In March 1971, the new Lakeland store opened to shoppers. Employees helped move contents from the old location into the newer one, and Tampa buyers came to Lakeland to supervise the displays. (Courtesy of Lakeland Public Library.)

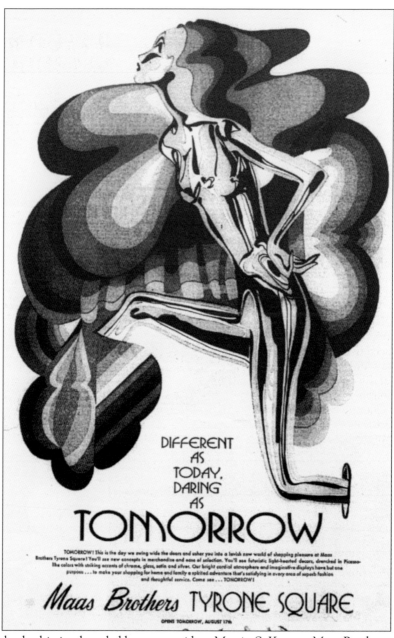

With new leadership in place, led by new president Martin S. Kramer, Maas Brothers continued its march to the suburbs and throughout Florida's West Coast. By 1970, the company completed plans and designs for its next shopping mall store at Tyrone Square in St. Petersburg. The Tyrone Square store opened on August 17, 1972, and sported a "futuristic and spirited" interior. Mickey Mouse was on hand to cut the ribbon, but an overcrowded store taxed the escalator banks. The opening had all of the pomp that surrounded shopping mall openings of the time. The *St. Petersburg Times* reported, "For a connoisseur of new places, a department store's grand opening has all the excitement of opening night on Broadway; for the compulsive shopper, a new store is enough reason to spend money; and for many people, being among the first inside a new building is a status symbol."

Bradenton was the next location for Maas Brothers, located at the new DeSoto Square Mall. Opened on August 15, 1973, it was the company's fifth shopping mall store. Maas parent Allied Stores was overwhelmed by the 110,000-square-foot store's response and announced that it was "just the addition the people of this area needed." (Courtesy of Manatee County Public Library.)

Bradenton's DeSoto Square Mall had all of the regular trappings and store offerings of a standard 1970s shopping mall. Maas Brothers had planned the Bradenton store back in 1970. Due to its popularity, the Bradenton store put stress on the longtime downtown Sarasota store. Sales figures at the Sarasota store were further challenged when the company opened its Sarasota Square location, in south Sarasota, on August 4, 1977. With the opening of Sarasota Square, Maas Brothers advertised, "Now we're twice as happy to call you home."

Maas Brothers continued its growth and built a store at Clearwater's Countryside Mall. Located in the first two-story enclosed shopping mall on Florida's West Coast, it opened on July 24, 1975. The store put strain on the older downtown Clearwater store, but the move was necessary in order to address increased shopping competition in the area. It was one of the first stores that opened in the mall, but the complex soon became one of the area's destination centers.

As the company promised, Maas Brothers continued to open a new store every year in order to reach customers, freshen its image, and address increased competition. In August 1974, University Square opened in North Tampa. The store's popularity was particularly increased due to its proximity to the University of South Florida. The major stores at University Square included Robinson's of Florida, J.C. Penney, Sears, and in 1983, Burdines. The University Square Mall Maas Brothers store met the shopping needs of loyal Maas shoppers who no longer desired to shop in downtown Tampa.

A collection of advertisements from 1976 shows some of the various offerings at Maas Brothers, including a complete car-care center at the West Shore Plaza location.

Five

MAAS BROTHERS, OF COURSE

The founders of department stores often became community leaders and important philanthropists. The Maas family members championed organizations such as the Tampa Board of Trade, the Tampa Children's Home, the Kiwanis Club, the Rotary Club, the Elk's Lodge, and Congregation Schaaral Zedek, Tampa's first synagogue.

By the 1940s, American department stores provided entertainment in addition to shopping opportunities. Their display windows were imaginative and engaging, whether it was Christmastime or just an ordinary day of the year. Show windows were also designed to stop potential shoppers from walking past the store. The displays of unique wares and artistic creativity were community traditions.

Maas Brothers' windows were a Franklin Street destination in Tampa. Display windows frequently changed, along with interior decorations and signage. The company also maintained a visible presence in Tampa's Gasparilla Parade and at St. Petersburg's Festival of States. Other locations hosted special events featuring notable personalities and merchandise representatives. Celebrities such as Gloria Vanderbilt, Tommy Hilfiger, Debbie Reynolds, Peter Max, the chimp J. Fred Muggs, and Dr. Ruth appeared at the company's various sites. Fashion shows and special events such as Maas Days, the Blockbuster Sale, and the Super Sale rounded out Maas Brothers' popularity in the community.

Like most prominent department stores, Maas Brothers never shied away from public events. These promotions helped advertise the business and provided entertainment. This image shows the popularity of Maas Brothers' 1947 Fashionolia show. (Courtesy of the University of South Florida Library.)

As a prominent community business, Maas Brothers usually participated in Tampa's famous Gasparilla Parade. This image shows the Maas float in the 25th annual celebration on February 6, 1933. (Courtesy of the Tampa–Hillsborough County Public Library.)

Display windows were another form of entertainment, and Maas Brothers frequently changed its displays at the Tampa and St. Petersburg stores. This 1946 window is titled "Vitamins for Victory" and showed how vitamins, along with good food such as corn flakes, pimento cheese, eggs, and milk can build a person's strength. (Courtesy of the Tampa–Hillsborough County Public Library.)

Another window at the downtown Tampa store displayed Elizabeth Arden cosmetics—famous beauty essentials—available exclusively at Maas Brothers in Tampa. This elaborate display dates from 1946. (Courtesy of the Tampa–Hillsborough County Public Library.)

Besides its elaborate Christmas windows, the downtown Tampa store often promoted merchandise for children, in addition to public-service announcements and special events. One display, at left, discussed safety issues during back-to-school time. The window was sponsored by the Tampa Motor Club and featured a shirt for $2.98 and pants for $4.98. The other display, seen below, celebrated "America's Most Charming Child." An unidentified child, the winner of an essay contest in the *Sunday Mirror*, sat in the store's window. (Courtesy of the Tampa–Hillsborough County Public Library.)

A Paul Bunyon float passes the downtown Tampa Maas Brothers store during the 1956 children's Gasparilla Parade. On the right, the popular and exclusive Wolf Brothers clothing store, along with its signature logo, can be seen at Maas's Franklin Street corner. (Courtesy of the University of South Florida Library.)

Gasparilla events were frequently held throughout the city, and the February 1937 event was held at an outdoor stadium. Maas Brothers entered a musically themed float for 1937. This image is part of the famous Burgert Brothers Photographic Collection, which documents Tampa life throughout the mid-20th century. (Courtesy of the Tampa–Hillsborough County Public Library.)

Maas Brothers windows were no less ornate at the downtown St. Petersburg store. These seashore-themed windows promoted casual Selby shoes, especially its Styl-EEZ brand footwear. An additional sign reminded male customers of the exclusive Men's Grill located on the store's second floor. (Courtesy of the St. Petersburg Museum of History.)

Surrounded by wrapped presents, mannequins suggest that shoppers purchase millinery accessories for Christmas at the St. Petersburg store. The company promoted hat certificates as the perfect gift for the holidays. The sign reads, "You . . . in gay holiday wrappings . . . Gifts of Fashion, to give, to receive." (Courtesy of the St. Petersburg Museum of History.)

Fashion director Julie Artman was a staple at the St. Petersburg store. Artman helped design the display windows and participated in many special events. She was also responsible for coordinating the store's Saturday teenage fashion programs. In addition, she helped shoppers learn the latest fashion trends and maintained a visible profile. At right, Artman helps promote Maas Brothers' Summer Sunfest, casual fashions for easy living, while below, she is pictured on the store's signature moving stairs. Both photographs date from June 1962.

Department stores played a crucial and important role for soon-to-be-married couples. Women frequently went to these stores and chose gowns and registered for gifts. This photograph shows a group of women shopping for wedding clothing at Maas Brothers' Lakeland store. (Courtesy of Richard Stein.)

Citrus products and fruit shipping were popular services at many large retailers in Florida. These hard-to-obtain goods made the perfect gifts for out-of-town friends and relatives. Maas Brothers always carried these products, and this newspaper advertisement reminded shoppers, through its famous slogan, that they were available "at Maas Brothers, of course!" The saying was used for many years, as evidenced in the Lakeland sales promotion below that featured visits with Santa Claus. When executive vice president Chuck James reflects on his time at the store he says, "Was I glad to have made the decision to join Maas Brothers? Well, as our advertising headline always stated, MAAS BROTHERS, OF COURSE! Thanks for the memories."

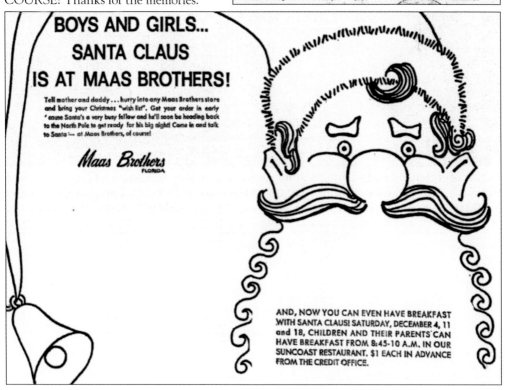

Just as Tampa had its annual Gasparilla Parade and festival, St. Petersburg had its springtime Festival of States. Maas Brothers frequently entered a float in the parade. Usually focused on Central Avenue, the St. Petersburg festival included participants from across the country. The parade had its final run in 2009. (Courtesy of the St. Petersburg Museum of History.)

The downtown Tampa store often featured a monthly Opportunity Day promotion that featured closeout items up to 50 percent off. This Opportunity Day advertisement is from October 1966. This sale, also held at the North Gate store, was especially important since it was held just days before the West Shore Plaza grand opening. The downtown store never recovered from the loss of customer traffic to West Shore. In 1966, the downtown main floor featured sportswear, junior sportswear, costume jewelry, handbags, fashion jewelry, men's sportswear and furnishings, candy, stationery, and village sportswear. The mezzanine housed men's clothing, books, and records. Better suits and coats, Junior Terrace, the Bridal Salon, Promenade Shop, women's vogue, Boulevard Room, millinery, and ladies' shoes were located on the Fashion Second Floor. The Thrift Mode Shop, boys' wear, and children's wear filled the third floor, while fabrics, linens, sewing notions, and lamps were on the fourth floor. The fifth floor was home to sporting goods, china and glassware, gifts, silverware, housewares, and The Closet Shop. Additional Opportunity Day values were found in the Clearwater, Lakeland, and Sarasota stores.

Maas Brothers was often noted for its restaurants and bakery counters. Most of its locations built up through the 1970s had some form of dining option. The bakery and candy were among the most popular departments at Maas Brothers.

In the 1960s, Maas Brothers featured its Gigantic World of Toys. The popular department carried "the newest toys, imported toys, the most unusual toys, and the most wanted toys." This advertisement from 1966 promoted tricycles, roly polies, walkie-talkies, and junior zithers.

Animated window displays were a mainstay at many department stores. They took months to build and involved considerable expense. Animated windows were a Christmas tradition that drew customers, and their children, to department stores. This image from the late 1960s shows children viewing a winter wonderland display at the St. Petersburg store. (Courtesy of the St. Petersburg Museum of History.)

By the late 1960s, display windows occasionally featured a space-age theme. This display at the St. Petersburg store portrayed Christmas on the moon. (Courtesy of the St. Petersburg Museum of History.)

Fashion shows were an obvious attraction at department stores. Often held in the store restaurants, these events featured members of the community as runway models. This photograph is from the 1977 Fall Fashion Show at the DeSoto Square store. (Courtesy of Manatee County Public Library.)

Maas Brothers sponsored a bicentennial float during the 1976 Gasparilla Parade in Tampa. That year was the company's 90th anniversary and the beginning of Frank Harvey's tenure as store president. This photograph, taken on February 9, 1976, showed the float as it wound its way through the downtown streets. The women on the float are dressed in some of the more popular fashions from the 1970s. (Courtesy of Manatee County Public Library.)

Six

MEETING THE COMPETITION

Maas Brothers was Tampa's big store, and no other came close to it in size or prominence. However, it was not entirely immune to competition. Franklin Street was home to numerous variety and specialty stores that provided quality and affordable goods. Wolf Brothers was Tampa's famous quality clothier, and its high-quality merchandise gave Maas Brothers some solid competition. O. Falk's, Tampa's other department store, did its best to offer a vast array of merchandise, and Haber's large apparel store maintained a visible presence just opposite Maas Brothers.

Maas Brothers thrived in St. Petersburg, where there was a lack of formidable retail competition. Willson-Chase Co., a "personable, first-class" retailer, was the city's closest resemblance to a downtown department store, but it was relatively small and incomplete. Rutland's, at Central at Fifth in the "Center of the Town," operated a popular multilevel apparel store until 1968. But the big St. Petersburg attraction was Webb's City. J.E. "Doc" Webb opened the "World's Most Unusual Drug Store" in 1924 and built it into a shopping and entertainment complex in the city's Central Plaza district. Busloads of curious shoppers were drawn to its talent and animal shows, in addition to its various offerings of goods. Nevertheless, Webb's City did not provide the comfortable and relaxed feeling of a traditional department store. Customers enjoyed that environment in Maas Brothers stores in Tampa, St. Petersburg, and throughout Florida's West Coast.

Franklin Street was the center of Tampa's commercial and social life. The street was lined with large and small businesses, theaters, and nearby hotels. Even when the stores were closed at night, crowds marveled at the display windows as a low cost form of entertainment. (Courtesy of the Tampa–Hillsborough County Public Library System.)

Maas Brothers was not the only large store in town, but it was arguably the most popular and complete. The second-largest store was O. Falk's, located on Franklin Street a block south of Maas Brothers. Founded in 1895, O. Falk's had a modest entrance on Franklin Street, and most of the building fronted Tampa Street. In reaction to Maas Brothers out-of-town owners, the Allied Stores Corporation, O. Falk's slogan was "Tampa Born, Tampa Owned, Tampa Managed." (Courtesy of the Tampa–Hillsborough County Public Library System.)

In 1930, David Falk became president of the store. He maintained a high profile in Tampa's business community and served as a former president of the Tampa Merchants' Association. O. Falk's carried everything from cosmetics on the main floor to carpets on the fifth floor. On the business side, O. Falk's did not have the money behind the business, and Maas Brothers often cherry-picked its best sales talent. It struggled to compete with Maas Brothers.

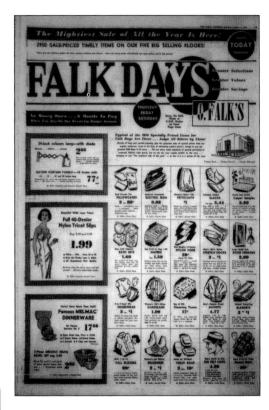

O. Falk's was sold and left family hands in the early 1960s. Its name was modernized to Falk's of Tampa. The company never opened any branch locations. As downtown lost its luster to the West Shore area, a business like Falk's lost its relevance. By 1971, Falk's of Tampa was no longer in operation.

prints, linens, shantungs

and more linens...

that's the story for this new spring season

and it's a season of great variety of style . . . there's the beltless princess line . . . the sheath dress . . . the full, full skirted dress . . . the jacket dress . . . the fabrics are beautiful, new, fascinating . . . the prices most reasonable . . .

see our Spring fashion show

sponsored by

DAVIS ISLANDS GARDEN CLUB

Tuesday evening, January 12th, 8:15 P. M.—Municipal Auditorium

admission $1.00

clothes for street, afternoon, evening . . . beachwear, shoes, hats, accessories

Wolf Brothers

woman's shop

Wolf Brothers was perhaps Tampa's premiere clothing store. Morris and Fred Wolf founded the business in 1898. The two brothers initially received their training at Maas Brothers. Wolf Brothers always maintained a close relationship with Maas Brothers. Abe Maas's wife was the former Bena Wolf. Wolf Brothers rarely had special sales and was known for its dignified advertisements. Wolf Brothers added locations throughout the state, and its signature Franklin Street store remained open until 1991. By 1996, its out-of-town owner, Hartmarx, closed the stores and ended a Tampa tradition.

An apology for the sale we cannot have

This is sale time. Each year about now when the Fall season is on the wane and new Spring suits are being unpacked, we clear away the small remainders of the old season to make room for the new. It makes good sense. Customers get a nice bargain—which is good for them. We clear away those one and two of a pattern that often remain after the season's active selling is over. That's good for us.

But, unfortunately, we can't announce a sale this season—even though we'd like to.

Strangely, although we have almost two hundred suits that might be offered, the sizes prevent it. There are practically no 39, 40, 41 and 42 regulars remaining. They are the most popular sizes—and it's better to call it all off rather than disappoint friends who would come in to find an inadequate selection. It just wouldn't be fair. It's too tough to leave business, find parking and then be greeted with—"sorry."

"Yes," you may say, "but I'm a size 46—and you've plenty for me." That's true. We've lots of shorts, too, and stouts and short stouts, long stouts and portlys. We've 35s and 50s, and those other less-popular sizes and proportions you find in a store like ours.

Maybe we can do it this way—

if you happen to be an unusual size—

And you've time to drop by with no harm done if it's just for the ride—

And if a savings of 20 to 30 percent would be of interest on a Fall weight suit of our best standard quality—

Then come in. We'll show what's here and do our level best to fit you, please you and give you a wonderful buy.

Wolf Brothers

Located across from Maas Brothers for over 50 years, Haber's was a popular multi-floor clothing department store. Over the years, Haber's opened other branches in Tampa and St. Petersburg. Haber's maintained a Franklin Street presence into the mid-1970s.

Another prominent area store was Belk-Lindsey, part of the Belk Stores Services Group in Charlotte, North Carolina. Belk-Lindsey expanded into Florida by way of Ocala and eventually made its way to Ybor City. The Britton Plaza Belk-Lindsey store in South Tampa was a shopping institution. Belk-Lindsey opened its Britton Plaza store on January 1, 1961, and closed in late 1993. A number of smaller Belk-Lindseys operated in the Tampa Bay area for a number of years.

Even though Tampa was perceived as a center of commerce, St. Petersburg enjoyed an active community and downtown shopping core. Central Avenue was lined with local and national retailers, along with green benches for its shoppers and visitors. The Rutland Building was a downtown landmark. Downtown's only department store, Willson-Chase Co., can be seen at far right. (Courtesy of the Florida State Archives.)

Willson-Chase was founded in 1909 and was St. Petersburg's closest resemblance to a large department store. It lacked a complete assortment and concentrated its offerings on apparel. It housed a special French room for exclusive designer goods. Willson-Chase and apparel-based Rutland's were St. Petersburg's largest downtown stores. Both welcomed Maas Brothers to the city but succumbed in the 1960s; Rutland's left downtown in 1968, and Willson-Chase closed in 1965. Willson-Chase became Joseph's department store but closed in the early 1970s.

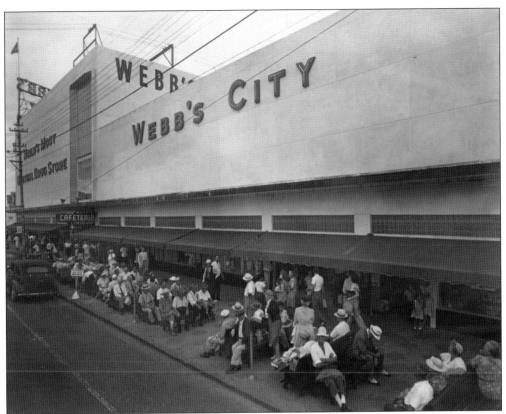

In 1925, J.E. "Doc" Webb began his retail empire at Ninth Street and First Avenue South. His business evolved into the "World's Most Unusual Drug Store" and became a shopping destination and attraction. Webb's City's sprawling complex offered entertainment, low prices, and acres of parking. It tried to fill any shopping voids from the downtown stores. When Maas Brothers came to St. Petersburg in 1948, Webb's City spruced up its stores and tried to address the new competitor. But Webb's City was unable to attract the moderate-to-better customer at Maas Brothers. Webb's City served the area until 1979, the victim of changing retail trends and increased discount competition. (Courtesy of the Florida State Archives.)

WEBB'S CITY'S
March of Progress

—— WHAT THE "HAMMERS" ACCOMPLISHED IN 1947! ——

- Built Three New Buildings (one five stories high!).
- Remodeled And Rebuilt All Old Buildings.
- Opened New Trading Post And Service Station.
  (TIRES, ACCESSORIES, FISHING TACKLE, PAINTS, SPORTING GOODS)
- Opened New Shoe Repair Shop.
- Opened New Family Shoe Store.
- A New Men's Furnishings Store
- Installed New, Complete Stainless Steel Plant To Make
  Webb's Double-Rich Ice Cream.
- Installed New 160 Foot Stainless Steel Soda Fountain With
  Complete Luncheon Facilities For 350 Persons
- Opened New Jewelry, Watch And Optical Store.
- Completely Remodeled Main Floor Drug Area.

COMPLETE NEW DEPARTMENT STORE—

SECOND AND THIRD FLOORS. A NEW BUILDING, NEW FIXTURES,
AND NEW TYPES OF MERCHANDISE!

Nationally Known Important People · · · Manufacturers, Merchants, Writers, Who Came From All Over America To Webb's Preview Of The Second Floor Say · · · It Is Beyond Doubt "America's Most Beautiful And Spacious Fashion Center"

WEBB'S NEW DEPARTMENT STORE
Is Serviced With

NEW OTIS ELEVATORS AND ESCALATORS!
The Only Otis Escalators in Central Florida And The West Coast

Webb's City Is The Nation's Most Famous Retail Store!!
More Than 500 Articles In 47 Newspapers, Trade Journals, Sunday Supplements, Etc.

YOU—
The Customers—Are Responsible For Our
Growth, By Your Patronage,
You Even Loaned Us The Money
with Which To Build!
We Will Show Our Appreciation

LENGTHY ARTICLES AND COLOR PHOTOS IN
"COLLIERS" AND "HOLIDAY"
AND A PAGES AND COLOR PHOTOS IN

PAGES 8 AND 9

JANUARY "FORTUNE" MAGAZINE!

WEBB'S CITY

By 1973, Maas Brothers' dominance in the moderate-to-better department-store market began to be challenged. Even though Sears and Montgomery Ward were always significant retail factors in the Tampa Bay market, newer retailers tried taking a bite out of Maas Brothers' market share. Robinson's of Florida, a new division developed by retailer Associated Dry Goods, opened its first location in 1973 at Tyrone Square. In 1974, the Clearwater Mall opened with retail newcomers Charlotte-based Ivey's, Montgomery, Alabama-based Gayfers, and Miami-based Burdines to the area. Maas Brothers did not ignore the competition, but customer loyalty kept the business intact. A study in the *Tampa Tribune* showed that 23 percent of all adults in Hillsborough County held Maas Brothers credit cards. The Gayfers store at the Clearwater Mall is pictured here. Gayfers was unable to satisfy the fashion needs of the Tampa Bay and never expanded further in the area.

Seven

FACING THE FUTURE

Maas Brothers entered the 1980s on seemingly solid footing even though the department-store industry was in flux. Reckless mergers affected morale and profit expectations for many retailers. But Maas Brothers continued to reach corporate milestones during this time. In 1985, Maas Brothers assumed control of Levy's in Savannah, another Allied Stores division. The year 1986 was the company's 100th anniversary. Maas Brothers celebrated in grand style and received national coverage.

In 1987, Allied Stores was sold to Canadian real estate developer Robert Campeau in a deal based on junk bonds and unrealistic sales projections. Campeau quickly pulled Allied apart, and his stores suffered from his misdirection. Campeau merged the struggling Miami-based Jordan Marsh stores into the profitable Maas Brothers division. Employee responsibilities practically doubled overnight, and in 1989, the stores were officially renamed Maas Brothers/Jordan Marsh. In addition, Campeau had acquired Federated Department Stores, the parent company of Burdines, in 1988. With Maas Brothers, Jordan Marsh, and Burdines all part of the same company, the business was renamed Federated Stores Inc. It was a massive burden to its Canadian owner, and his new company was unsustainable.

Maas Brothers' downtown Tampa location felt the effects of the city's white flight and economic shift to suburban areas. It maintained its status as the headquarters store, but the size of its selling space was constantly reduced. Lisa Lichtenberg recalls, "As the company grew, the store was eaten away because we needed the space for all of the offices." By the late 1970s, the store was reduced to only three selling floors, but it maintained a loyal clientele. (Courtesy of the St. Petersburg Museum of History.)

With ample parking and late-night hours in the suburbs, the downtown Tampa location was no longer considered the flagship store. "West Shore became our premiere store," says Lisa Lichtenberg. "It did the highest volume and presented special events such as movie star visits."

Ron Rodriguez was vice president of special events and organized many celebrity appearances. He says that Eva Gabor had a wonderful sense of humor and loved pets. "At an appearance at West Shore, she was wearing a white floor-length fur coat but then saw a six-week old boxer puppy. She held it in her arms kissing it and I just prayed that the puppy wouldn't have an accident! We traveled by limo to another store and stopped for lunch by the water. The first thing Miss Gabor does is start feeding the gulls. It looked like a scene out of *The Birds*!" Gloria Vanderbilt was also one of Rodriguez's favorite celebrities. "She is a wonderful person and a class act." Pictured here is Ron Rodriguez during appearances with Gabor and Vanderbilt. (Both, courtesy of Ron Rodriguez.)

By 1975, Tampa's Franklin Street resembled a ghost town. O. Falk's was demolished and the J.C. Penney Co., shown here as the Stratford Women's College, had closed. Franklin Street had transitioned into a pedestrian shopping street, without pedestrians or automobiles. Besides a few smaller stores, only the Wolf Brothers and Maas Brothers stores remain as the city's largest downtown retailers. (Courtesy of the Florida State Archives.)

Many of the Maas Brothers stores thrived in their locations, and the division was considered the darling of the Allied Stores Corporation. However, in addition to the aging and rambling downtown Tampa store, other locations were showing some wear. The above photograph shows the Maas Brothers store at the Gainesville Mall in its later years. The store maintained a strong business, but the center struggled to compete with the newer Oaks Mall. The uptown Sarasota store is seen at right. The store tried to rebound and became part of the adjoining Main Plaza shopping mall.

Maas Brothers moved farther inland in February 1977 when it took over the lease of a former Britt's department store in Winter Haven. The Britt's store, a former division of J.J. Newberry, was only 60,000 square feet. Another small location at the Coastland Center in Naples opened that February. Store president Frank Harvey said the Naples store "featured a primary emphasis on ready-to-wear fashions that reflected the Florida lifestyle."

A slightly larger store was built at the Gulfview Square Mall in New Port Richey. Opened on August 21, 1981, the Gulfview Square store was the most northern store in the Tampa Bay market and served customers in Pasco and Hernando Counties. The store was similar in size and design to the Paddock Mall Maas Brothers in Ocala. The Paddock Mall store opened in August 1980 and praised the community by saying, "We think your life is just our style, Ocala."

Port Richey: your life is our style.

Maas Brothers

Opening Saturday, August 22 at Gulfview Square Mall.

The farthest store from Tampa Bay opened in August 1979 at Governor's Square Mall in Tallahassee. Maas Brothers saw this move as a potential opportunity to open more locations throughout the state. Though the location was relatively successful, the Tallahassee store remained the company's only location in the state's Panhandle. This photograph depicts an interior display at the Tallahassee store. (Courtesy of the Florida State Archives.)

This photograph shows the cosmetics counter at the Bradenton Maas Brothers in 1978. This counter featured the Estée Lauder line of products. (Courtesy of Manatee County Public Library.)

From that day, one hundred years ago, the company's history is one of ever expanding to make room for the large following that began with the country people who took a personal interest in the man who started it all.

Sidney H. Levy & Arthur B. Levy admitted to membership in the firm in 1904.

On February 29, 1904, Arthur B. Levy and Sidney H. Levy were admitted as members of the firm to be known as B. H. Levy, Bros., & Co. The young men, sons of Benjamin and Henry, had been with the business for some years and were familiar with its details. During this time the store delt exclusively with men's and boy's clothing and furnishings.

Benjamin H. Levy
Founder and chief

The modest little shop on Bryan Street opened by B. H. Levy on August 26, 1871

Henry Levy - The financial manager entered the firm in 1878.

1971, present home of Levy's of S

FIRST HUNDRED YEAR

In 1871, Benjamin H. Levy opened a modest store in downtown Savannah, Georgia. Over the years, Levy's of Savannah grew and became one of the city's largest retailers. Allied Stores Corporation, the parent of Maas Brothers, purchased Levy's in 1947. Its downtown store was enlarged and renovated in 1954. In 1982, Levy's built a suburban store at the Oglethorpe Mall,

1871 ⟨&⟩ 1972 FOR⋯

Levy's OF SAVANNAH

With a century behind it, Levy's of Savannah is enjoying the prosperity that was the dream of its French imigrant founder. Behind a modern facade of glass at 201 East Broughton Street, lies thousands of square feet of theme oriented displays of retail merchandise. The present location of Levy's is quite a contrast to the original store operated by Benjamin H. Levy in 1871, known as "B.H. Levy, General Merchandise, Bryan and Jefferson Streets."

With an unbroken history of a century of business prosperity and service, Levy's of Savannah is firmly established in the Coastal Empire as a firm founded on integrity.

SIEGFRIED LAHM
PRESIDENT AND MANAGING DIRECTOR

THE SECOND HUNDRED YEARS FOR LEVY'S DEPARTMENT STORE IS BEING LAUNCHED WITH GREAT EXPECTATIONS UNDER THE DYNAMIC LEADERSHIP OF MR. SIGFRIED LAHM AS ITS PRESIDENT AND MANAGING DIRECTOR.

A NATIVE OF SALSBURG, AUSTRIA, MR. LAHM ATTENDED HIGH SCHOOL IN MANSFIELD, OHIO AND GRADUATED FROM WITTENBERG UNIVERSITY IN 1961 WITH A B.S. DEGREE IN BUSINESS ADMINISTRATION AND ECONOMICS. SOON AFTER HIS GRADUATION HE JOINED WREN'S DEPARTMENT STORE IN SPRINGFIELD, OHIO, AN ALLIED STORE. DURING THE FOLLOWING YEARS HE HELD VARIOUS POSITIONS UNTIL HE WAS PROMOTED TO BE ITS VICE PRESIDENT IN 1969. HE WAS A MEMBER OF SPRINGFIELD CHAMBER OF COMMERCE AND HELD POSITION AS PRESIDENT OF SPRINGFIELD DOWNTOWN MERCHANTS ASSOCIATION.

Levy's location in 1921.

SECOND HUNDRED YEARS

Savannah—December 21

which was modeled after Maas Brothers' New Port Richey and Ocala locations. In an effort to reduce expenses, the small Levy's division was merged into Allied's Maas Brothers stores in February 1986. On a historical note, the father of former Maas chairman Jerome Waterman's brother-in-law founded Levy's of Savannah.

In June 1978, Marilyn Gallock served as manager for the day at the Maas Brothers store in Bradenton's DeSoto Square Mall. In these photographs, Gallock oversaw the store's cosmetic, sportswear, and home departments. Most locations hosted a customer advisory board. Maas Brothers assembled women from clubs and various organizations to offered assistance with merchandise selections and service improvements. Customer advisory boards often held monthly meetings. With such events as manager of the day, some participants learned that store leadership cannot control everything in a department store. (Both, courtesy of Manatee County Public Library.)

Maas Brothers 100 Year Gala
January 20, 1986

On January 20, 1986, Maas Brothers celebrated its 100th anniversary in style and threw a black-tie gala at the Tampa Hyatt Regency. Comedian Alan King, 850 business associates and executives, Skitch Henderson, and members of the Florida Orchestra celebrated the company's milestone. The five-hour gala was a fitting tribute for the beloved store. (Courtesy if Lisa Lichtenberg.)

The year 1986 marked 100 years of quality for Maas Brothers. Its 100th birthday was celebrated on the *Today* show with Willard Scott. However, by the end of the year, the celebratory mood at Maas Brothers waned. Retail mergers were at their peak, and Robert Campeau, a French Canadian real estate developer, made an unsolicited offer for Allied Stores on September 4, 1986. Initially rejected by the Allied board, Campeau purchased Allied Stores the following October for $3.3 billion. It was $900 million greater than his initial hostile bid. But the purchase included hefty unrealistic debt payments. Campeau promised to reduce expenses by 20 percent and increase sales by 20 percent. He had grand plans for his new stores and convinced Wall Street to stand by him. The man who made his own private withdrawals at the store cash office and who had his own person follow him about the store with a bag of oranges ("Mr. Campeau refuses to drink orange juice from concentrate.") was set to usher Maas Brothers into a new era, fraught with problems. (Courtesy of the University of South Florida Library.)

Eight

MAKING CLOSURE

On January 15, 1990, Maas Brothers' parent company, Federated Stores Inc., filed for Chapter 11 bankruptcy. The interest on the debt alone was too much for the new owner, Robert Campeau. Creditors demanded a suitable reorganization, and massive cuts and closures were imminent. Florida's Maas Brothers/Jordan Marsh and Burdines divisions appeared redundant, and the company braced for changes.

On February 4, 1991, Campeau announced the closure of the downtown Tampa Maas Brothers. The store was a shell of its former self and had been threatened with closure over the past several years, in spite of a small loyal clientele and popularity with downtown workers. The Tampa location was not the only store affected. The longtime downtown Sarasota store and two Burdines locations were eliminated in March and the downtown Clearwater store was closed shortly afterwards.

Megan Weber, the store's final operations manager, recalls the last years in downtown Tampa. "I remember the time a homeless woman fell asleep on one of the booths in the lunch room on a Friday and spent the weekend in the store. Also, the day the health inspector walked right into the grease trap, and how I barged into J. David Scheiner's board meeting soaking wet looking for leaks, after spending time on the roof in the rainstorm." General operating manager Robert Anderson simply commented, "As a child it had seemed so big. It had the first escalator in Florida. I used to love to ride it. Upon my return [from the Army], everything downtown seemed so small to me and the escalator seemed so narrow."

The store closures did not end in Tampa, Sarasota, and Clearwater. On July 8, 1991, the 280-employee headquarters staff was notified that all jobs would be eliminated on September 7. In August, the once-iconic downtown St. Petersburg store announced its final sale. The remaining Maas Brothers stores were converted to Burdines on October 20, 1991, and the Maas Brothers name became a part of retailing history.

The effects of Robert Campeau's 1986 purchase of Allied Stores were felt the most at the downtown Tampa corporate headquarters. Soon after the 100th-anniversary gala, Maas Brothers contracted with an offsite black-mirrored office building as its new headquarters. The planned move accompanied a February 1987 announcement that the downtown store would close within two years.

Though the scene outside the Tampa store was quiet, the corporate headquarters inside the building remained active, despite concerns regarding its new owner. According to Sue Meadows, "A lovely coffee lady named Gussie would wheel a cart from floor to floor. As she arrived on each floor, she'd ring a bell and shout, 'Gussie's here!' That was our cue. She was so stylish, even in her white uniform, and wore large rhinestone earrings with a turned up collar."

The downtown Tampa store was a shadow of its former self but well maintained and still modestly profitable. It also kept its display-window tradition alive. Even though area leaders commented on its "layers of dirty grit and drab coats of paint," historians praised its significance and regarded it as a diamond in the rough. Several plans were made to restore and rebuild the downtown building once Maas Brothers vacated it.

Soon after he purchased Allied, Robert Campeau decided to merge the Miami-based Jordan Marsh division into Maas Brothers. Jordan Marsh Florida was a division Allied built from the ground up in 1956. Originally, it was loosely tied to the Jordan Marsh Boston stores, but its working partnership quickly diminished. When the division was founded, it challenged Miami's Burdines as a fashion leader but lost its luster over the years. This is an early image of the original downtown Miami Jordan Marsh store.

A 1980s Christmastime shopping bag uses both the Maas Brothers and Jordan Marsh nameplates in its design.

In January 1987, Mass Brothers immediately assumed the buying and administrative responsibilities of the Jordan Marsh East Coast stores. The 21-store Maas Brothers division grew overnight into a 38-store company. The takeover of Jordan Marsh cost more than 300 administrative jobs at its Miami offices. This image of the downtown Miami store shows its newly renamed Suncoast Restaurant.

According to Lisa Lichtenberg, Maas Brothers' director of merchandise information, "Jordan Marsh [Florida] never ever was the success that Maas Brothers was." This photograph shows its Miami International Mall location in 1991.

Robert Campeau continued on his buying spree. He convinced Wall Street to loan him even more to acquire Federated Department Stores, Burdines' parent, in April 1988. Federated was the parent of Bloomingdale's, one of Campeau's purchase prizes. Ron Rodriguez recalls driving Robert Campeau around while visiting stores. "[Robert] asked, 'Do I have a store in Palm Beach?' and I said, 'Do you want one?'" The downtown Miami Burdines is pictured here in 1991.

CONGRATULATIONS TO
THE SAVANNAH SYMPHONY

Jordan Marsh
THE TRADITION CONTINUES

Oglethorpe Mall, Savannah
The Mall at Shelter Cove, Hilton Head

Director of stores Talbot Boudreau reported that Levy's Savannah stores "didn't make much money" and "didn't do as well as they should. Levy's would never carry the right merchandise." In an effort to reduce costs, Campeau shed many Allied store divisions and closed marginally profitable stores. The downtown Savannah Maas Brothers, formerly Levy's, was closed on December 31, 1987.

After the downtown Savannah Maas Brothers store was shuttered, the company gave the other two Savannah-area stores the Jordan Marsh nameplate. This included the Oglethorpe Mall branch and the newly-built store on Hilton Head Island, South Carolina. Store officials felt that the Jordan Marsh name would be more popular and identifiable to Savannah and Hilton Head shoppers. Jordan Marsh remained supportive of local Savannah organizations, including the Savannah Symphony Orchestra.

This photograph shows the interior of the former downtown Savannah store during a Festival of Trees celebration. The location now serves as the library for the Savannah College of Art and Design.

The downtown Savannah store displayed Christmas signage well after its 1987 closure.

By mid-1989, Campeau struggled to pay his hundreds of millions of dollars in overdue bills and debt payments from his purchase of Allied and Federated. Vendors and manufacturers were advised to hold off on deliveries until a payment plan was reached. Campeau's troubles jeopardized his large collection of Florida stores: Maas Brothers, Jordan Marsh, and Burdines. On January 15, 1990, Campeau filed for Chapter 11 bankruptcy protection. His reckless purchase of Allied and Federated jeopardized the country's department-store industry. Employees, executives, and shoppers waited to see what effect the bankruptcy would have on his almost 400 stores. These two images show the quiet downtown Tampa store in August 1989, during the height of Campeau's troubles. In 1989, as Campeau's fortunes faded, his company reversed its plans to move the offices out of the Tampa store and remained downtown.

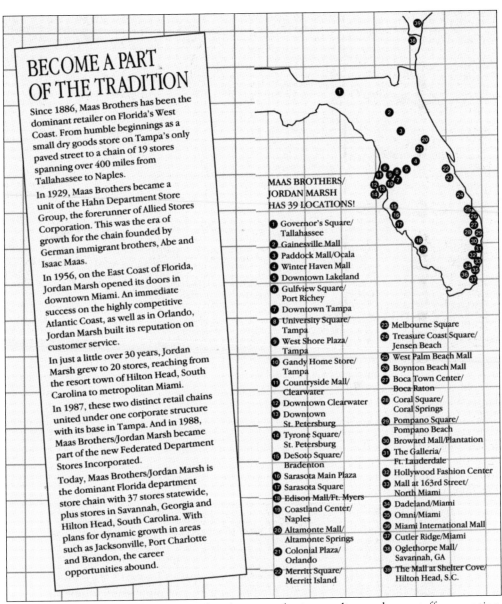

BECOME A PART OF THE TRADITION

Since 1886, Maas Brothers has been the dominant retailer on Florida's West Coast. From humble beginnings as a small dry goods store on Tampa's only paved street to a chain of 19 stores spanning over 400 miles from Tallahassee to Naples.

In 1929, Maas Brothers became a unit of the Hahn Department Store Group, the forerunner of Allied Stores Corporation. This was the era of growth for the chain founded by German immigrant brothers, Abe and Isaac Maas.

In 1956, on the East Coast of Florida, Jordan Marsh opened its doors in downtown Miami. An immediate success on the highly competitive Atlantic Coast, as well as in Orlando, Jordan Marsh built its reputation on customer service.

In just a little over 30 years, Jordan Marsh grew to 20 stores, reaching from the resort town of Hilton Head, South Carolina to metropolitan Miami.

In 1987, these two distinct retail chains united under one corporate structure with its base in Tampa. And in 1988, Maas Brothers/Jordan Marsh became part of the new Federated Department Stores Incorporated.

Today, Maas Brothers/Jordan Marsh is the dominant Florida department store chain with 37 stores statewide, plus stores in Savannah, Georgia and Hilton Head, South Carolina. With plans for dynamic growth in areas such as Jacksonville, Port Charlotte and Brandon, the career opportunities abound.

MAAS BROTHERS/JORDAN MARSH HAS 39 LOCATIONS!

1 Governor's Square/ Tallahassee
2 Gainesville Mall
3 Paddock Mall/Ocala
4 Winter Haven Mall
5 Downtown Lakeland
6 Gulfview Square/ Port Richey
7 Downtown Tampa
8 University Square/ Tampa
9 West Shore Plaza/ Tampa
10 Gandy Home Store/ Tampa
11 Countryside Mall/ Clearwater
12 Downtown Clearwater
13 Downtown St. Petersburg
14 Tyrone Square/ St. Petersburg
15 DeSoto Square/ Bradenton
16 Sarasota Main Plaza
17 Sarasota Square
18 Edison Mall/Ft. Myers
19 Coastland Center/ Naples
20 Altamonte Mall/ Altamonte Springs
21 Colonial Plaza/ Orlando
22 Merritt Square/ Merritt Island
23 Melbourne Square
24 Treasure Coast Square/ Jensen Beach
25 West Palm Beach Mall
26 Boynton Beach Mall
27 Boca Town Center/ Boca Raton
28 Coral Square/ Coral Springs
29 Pompano Square/ Pompano Beach
30 Broward Mall/Plantation
31 The Galleria/ Ft. Lauderdale
32 Hollywood Fashion Center
33 Mall at 163rd Street/ North Miami
34 Dadeland/Miami
35 Omni/Miami
36 Miami International Mall
37 Cutler Ridge/Miami
38 Oglethorpe Mall/ Savannah, GA
39 The Mall at Shelter Cove/ Hilton Head, S.C.

Though they had combined their merchandising, marketing, credit, warehouse staff, accounting, and various other departments, Maas Brothers and Jordan Marsh maintained their separate nameplates. On August 11, 1989, Pres. David Scheiner officially announced that the new name of stores, as of August 20, would be changed to Maas Brothers/Jordan Marsh.

On February 4, 1991, the first axe fell at Maas Brothers when Campeau announced that the downtown Tampa and Sarasota stores would close by March 31. Employees of the downtown Tampa store posed for this final photograph outside the iconic store. Pictured are, from left to right, (first row) Carolyn Thomas, MaryRose Noto, Lil Machado, Annie "Gussie" Clark, Rosemary Hazelton, Nina Lahey, Chris Gitelson, Dot Ferguson, Alice Lamarco, Grace Claridge, David Claridge, and Oscar Sanchez; (second row) Dorothy "Dottie" Smith, Liz Lawson, Mary Primm, Fannie Mae Harris-Jones, James Prather, Jeaneen Riches, Ginny Krisky, Alberta Blake, Valerie Wallace, Signe McClendon, and Susie Sims. (third row) Megan Weber, Lucille Anthony, Willie, Nealy, Audrey Roberts, Dot Issler, Darlene Carter, Judy Perez, Ann Stewart, Larry Rodgers, Sharon Andrews, Shirley Harris, Joyce Pierce, Wanda Singfield, Michelle Barnett, Yvonne Mathis, Barbara Smith, Sophia Ventura, Linda Darnes, Jackie Oden, and Kathy Burney. (Courtesy of Megan Weber.)

The final closing sale at the downtown Tampa location began on March 8, 1991. The store finally closed on March 23, 1991.

At the time of the Tampa closing sale, other locations participated in the popular Super Sale promotion.

In April 1991, the downtown Clearwater Maas Brothers was put up for sale, along with the University Mall and Crossroads Burdines stores. The Clearwater store had been an area landmark since 1961. However, its waterfront property was an extremely valuable asset. City officials had been interested in buying the property for years, and the parent company's financial crisis provided a lucrative opportunity.

After months of speculation, Maas Brothers' newly organized parent, Federated Stores Inc., announced the closing of the Maas Brothers/Jordan Marsh division headquarters. The closure affected about 250 merchandise buyers and 30 marketing and advertising employees. Some of the employees were offered similar positions at the Burdines division, but most received severance pay or refused to relocate to Miami and leave Tampa.

One of the final blows to the Maas Brothers legacy was the final closing of the downtown St. Petersburg store. On August 3, the company stated its intention to close the 1948 department store by early October. The announcement was a blow to the city's downtown, since Maas Brothers was integral to the proposed Bay Plaza redevelopment. Director of stores Talbot Boudreau reflected, "I was so sorry to see that we had to leave that store." Pres. Jerome Waterman initially hired Boudreau to write a daily report on the store's progress during its 1948 opening. Boudreau's onsite reports earned him a $5 a week bonus.

The St. Petersburg announcement coincided with the proposed sale and closure of several Jordan Marsh stores on Florida's East Coast. This image shows the Pompano Beach Jordan Marsh location.

Pink Slip Party
August 23, 1991

On Friday, August 23, 1991, the Tampa central office employees held a pink-slip party at the Davis Island Garden Club. The party invitation stated, "Your presence is requested at one final meeting." The agenda included an open bar, lots of food, loud music, and hilarious entertainment. (Courtesy of Lisa Lichtenberg.)

On October 2, 1991, the St. Petersburg location closed for good. The 278,000-square-foot store had operated on the Sunshine Corner for almost 44 years. Once considered a flagship store, Maas Brothers' 700-person sales force had dropped to 135 in its later years. The St. Petersburg store once carried fabric, paint, gourmet foods, refrigerators, sheds, records, a Budget Shop, and Chris the Talking Christmas Tree.

The Maas Brothers legacy officially ended when all remaining locations were folded into the Burdines nameplate. The name change occurred on October 20, 1991, and Burdines grew into a 45-store operation. Burdines spent about $3 million over the next several months and removed all former Maas Brothers/Jordan Marsh signage. These photographs shows the now-closed Gainesville Mall store operating as a Burdines.

Even though it was popular and profitable, Burdines was not immune to a name change. Federated Stores Inc. acquired the Macy's name in 1992 and saw the value in creating a national department-store brand. The company initially used the Burdines-Macy's name until it dropped the Burdines name in 2005. These images show the downtown Miami store as it worked its way through the name changes.

The first Maas Brothers Central Office Reunion occurred on April 27, 2013, at the Tampa Bay History Center. The event drew hundreds of former central-office workers who reflected on their time at Tampa's once-dominant retailer. The members of the reunion committee were Ruthie Smith Rorebeck, Lisa Lichtenberg, and Carol Gaynor. (Courtesy of Lisa Lichtenberg.)

General operating manager Robert Anderson simply said, "I have been in real estate since I left and even today when people find I was there they always tell me a story of their love for Maas Brothers and how much they miss it. Somehow life has never been the same for most of us who had the privilege of working in that wonderful family. We were blessed." (Courtesy of Lisa Lichtenberg.)

Pave Paradise,
Put Up a Parking Lot!

In October 1998, members of the Maas family, known as the Maas Bros. Beneficiary Trust, sold the Tampa building for $1.5 million. The structure was demolished eight years later. Former director of merchandise information Lisa Lichtenberg reflected on the demolition of the historic downtown Tampa Maas Brothers building. "It was 2006, a beautiful Saturday in early March for the Gasparilla Art Festival in downtown Tampa. After parking my car and crossing the street I looked up to see a crane with a giant wrecking ball destroying the building where I'd spent 10 years of my career . . . there had been no fanfare, no announcements in the TV news or newspaper, and my heart stuck in my throat. After over 100 years the Maas Brothers building was being destroyed to make way for a parking lot. "They paved paradise, put up a parking lot!" (Courtesy of Lisa Lichtenberg.)

The Neptune Room

MAAS BROTHERS
TAMPA, FLORIDA

Most Maas Brothers stores included dining rooms that catered to hungry shoppers and encouraged customers not to leave their doors. The Neptune Room in downtown Tampa and the Imperial Room in downtown Lakeland were two signature Maas Brothers restaurants.

The Imperial Room

MAAS BROTHERS
LAKELAND, FLORIDA

Nine

FINE DINING

Whether people remembered them as the Neptune Room, the Sunshine Room, the Imperial Room, or simply the Suncoast Restaurant, Maas Brothers created a complete shopping experience with its popular in-store dining rooms. These restaurants were rarely profitable for the company, but they were an essential part of a department store's business practice. Successful retailers needed to keep their customers comfortable, entertained, and well fed. The popularity of Maas's in-store restaurants kept shoppers from leaving the store in search of food or a break. The Maas Brothers' restaurants, regarded for their food, service, and special events, helped make the company a Florida West Coast tradition.

Many people still equate Maas Brothers with their popular cinnamon twists. It was a signature offering that brought customers back to the store time after time. It has become clear that these popular and personal local department stores will not return. Business and social trends have passed them by, but some of the more-popular Maas Brothers recipes are included on the following pages. It is not possible to shop at Maas Brothers anymore, but one can, with the help of the following recipes, have a cinnamon twist. The Maas Brothers tradition continues.

THE *Sunshine Room*
Maas Brothers
ST. PETERSBURG

The Sunshine Room restaurant was located on the St. Petersburg store's mezzanine and gave shoppers an overview of the main floor.

The Sunshine Room

The Sunshine Room

SATURDAY, JANUARY 19, 1957

LUNCHEON MENU
11:30 to 2:30

SALAD SUGGESTIONS

1. A Sunshine Fruit Plate of Fresh Winter
Fruits, Topped with Fluffy Orange
Dressing and Toasted Coconut — Garnished
with Fresh Strawberries — Served with a
Hot Pecan Honey Roll. 1.25

2. Sea Food Salad Bowl (Fresh Maine Lobster,
King Crab and Shrimp, Chopped Hard Cooked
Egg and Celery, Tangy Mustard Mayonnaise)
Garnished with Sweet Pickled Watermelon
Rind and a Black Olive. 1.15

3. For The Weight Watcher: Pineapple Rings
and Cottage Cheese with Watercress, A
Hot Blueberry Muffin 75

SANDWICHES

1. Cream Cheese, Shredded Turkey and Crispy
Bacon on Homemade Bread, Stuffed Olives
and Saratoga Chips. 60
Served with Frosted Orange and
Grapefruit Sections. 90

2. Baked Sugar Cured Ham and Imported Swiss
Cheese Sandwich on Homemade Rye Bread,
Cabbage Slaw with Russian Dressing,
Garnished with Pic-L-Joys. 85

3. Breast of Turkey and Crispy Bacon Sandwich
on Whole Wheat Bread with Celery Sticks
and Stuffed Olives. 1.00

BEVERAGES

Hot Coffee...10   A Pot of Tea...10
Iced Coffee...15   Iced Tea...10
Postum...15   Sanka...15
           Milk...15

FROM THE GRILL

Grilled Chopped Steak on a Toasted Roll,
Pic-L-Joys, Tomato and Deviled Egg Salad
1.00

TODAY'S SNACK

A Cup of Chicken and Noodle Soup Soup or
Frosted Fresh Fruit Cup, Assorted Tea
Sandwiches on Homemade Bread. 85

SEA FOOD SUGGESTION

Sea Food Au Gratin (Fresh Maine Lobster
and King Crab) A Salad. 1.35

DESSERTS

Fresh Strawberry Parfait...35
Frozen Ice Cream Eclair Topped with Hot Fudge Sauce.35
Coffee Hot Fudge Sundae...35
Lemon Filled Angel Cake Topped with Almond Fluff..30
Fudge Loaf Cake...20
Boston Cream Pie...15
Hot French Apple Pie, An Ice Cream Ball...30
Coconut Pie with Whipped Cream...25
Pumpkin Pie with Whipped Cream...25
Vanilla, Chocolate, Strawberry, Butter Pecan,
Coffee Ice Cream or Sherbet,
Served with a Tea Cookie...25

Twenty Minutes Will Be Required With All Grill Items

APPETIZERS

Frosted Fruit Juice..10 Fruit Cup Supreme...30
Fresh Shrimp Cocktail...65
Chicken and Noodle Soup .20

SHOPPERS! LUNCHEON SUGGESTIONS
Served with Hot Rolls and Butter

1. Strawberry Griddle Cakes with Maple Syrup
Crispy Bacon, Fresh Pear and Avocado Salad
with Watercress Dressing. 1.25

2. Italian Spaghetti with Meat Sauce, A
Green Salad with Italian Dressing. . . .95

3. Lamb Chop Grill (Broiled Loin Lamb Chop,
Sauteed Chicken Liver and Crisp Bacon
Strip) Baked Potato and Green Beans —
A Salad. 1.55

4. Luncheon Feature

Sliced Turkey over Savory Stuffing

Brown Gravy   Cranberries

Green Beans

Orange, Grapefruit and Avocado Salad

A Hot Roll

Pistachio Ice Cream and Chocolate Chiffon Cake
or
A Sherbet and Coconut Macaroon

1.55

No Substitutions Please

The menu of the St. Petersburg Sunshine Room from January 19, 1957, is pictured here.

Maas Brothers Cinnamon Twists

$^1/_2$ cup warm water
2 packages active dry yeast
2 eggs
$^1/_2$ cup warm milk
$^1/_2$ cup sugar
1 teaspoon salt
$^1/_2$ cup shortening
1 teaspoon vanilla extract
$4^1/_2$ to 5 cups all-purpose flour
$^1/_2$ cup melted butter
1 cup sugar
$2^1/_2$ tablespoons ground cinnamon

- Dissolve yeast in water. Add eggs, milk, sugar, salt, shortening, vanilla and $2^1/_2$ cups of the flour. Mix until creamy and smooth. Add enough flour to make dough easy to handle. Knead on floured board for five minutes. Put in greased bowl and cover. Let stand at room temperature 1.5 hours. Punch down. Let rise 30 minutes.
- Cut dough into two pieces. Roll out each piece to approximately 8 by 16 inches. Brush one side with melted butter. Mix sugar and cinnamon together; sprinkle over rectangles.
- Fold outer long edges of dough to center of strip. Repeat brushing with melted butter and sprinkle with cinnamon sugar mixture.
- Fold half of the dough the long way to the edge of the other half. There will now be four layers of dough approximately two inches wide. Roll out to a width of four inches.
- Cut a strip every $^3/_4$ of an inch. Each piece of dough is given one twist and placed in a shallow greased pan. Place each twist against each other.
- Brush tops of twists with melted butter and sprinkle with cinnamon-sugar mixture. Bake at 375 degrees Fahrenheit for 30 minutes. Makes about 40 twists.

Maas Brothers French Dressing

$^1/_2$ can tomato soup
$^1/_4$ cup sugar
$^1/_3$ cup white vinegar
$^3/_4$ cup oil
$^1/_2$ tablespoon garlic powder
$^1/_2$ teaspoon seasoned pepper
$^1/_4$ teaspoon onion powder
$^1/_4$ teaspoon paprika
$^1/_2$ teaspoon lemon juice

- Combine ingredients in a blender. Pulse on high about one minute. Pour into a bottle with a cap. Refrigerate.

Maas Brothers Florentine Salad

1 package lemon gelatin
1 cup boiling water
1 10-ounce package chopped spinach, (remove stems, wash, and chop leaves)
1 cup mayonnaise
1 cup cottage cheese, large curd
1/4 tablespoon vinegar
1/2 cup chopped celery
1 tablespoon chopped onion

- Dry the spinach well by squeezing it in paper towels. Dissolve gelatin in hot water. Chill until partially set. Add thawed raw spinach, mayonnaise, cottage cheese, vinegar, celery, and onion. Pour into a square pan, 2.25-inches deep, chill until set, and cut into squares. Serve on fresh greens and garnish with fresh fruit.

Fruit and Nut Cake

Cake:
5 eggs
1 teaspoon vanilla
1 cup sugar
1 cup flour
1/2 teaspoon baking powder
1/2 teaspoon salt

Filling:
1 8-ounce package cream cheese, softened
1 cup sugar, divided
1 teaspoon vanilla
1/4 teaspoon cinnamon
1 cup sour cream
1/2 cup finely chopped nuts
1/2 cup flaked coconut
1/3 cup chopped maraschino cherries
1/3 cup dates (optional)
2 (1.55-ounce) milk chocolate candy bars, shaved or finely chopped
1 1/2 cups whipping cream

- In a mixing bowl, beat eggs and vanilla on high until foamy. Add sugar; beat until mixture is thick and lemon-colored. Combine flour, baking powder, and salt; fold into egg mixture, a third at a time. Pour into two greased and floured nine-inch round cake pans. Bake at 350 degrees for 25 to 30 minutes or until cake springs back when lightly touched. Cool for five minutes; remove from pans to wire racks to cool completely.
- In a mixing bowl, beat cream cheese, 2/3 cup sugar, vanilla, and cinnamon until smooth. Stir in sour cream, nuts, coconut, cherries, and dates, if using. Fold in chocolate. Beat cream and remaining sugar. Fold half into cream cheese mixture.
- Split each cake into two horizontal layers; spread 1/4 of the cream cheese mixture on one layer. Repeat with the remaining three layers. Frost sides with reserved whipped cream. Refrigerate until serving time.

The matchbook at left promotes the former downtown Tampa Colonial Tea Room and Fountainette, while the one below, presumably from the late 1960s, lists the various Maas Brothers cities in Florida.

ABOUT THE AUTHOR

Michael Lisicky is a nationally recognized department-store historian, lecturer, and author. He has appeared on the CBS *Sunday Morning* television program, *Fortune* magazine, and National Public Radio. His books have been featured in the *Washington Post*, *Philadelphia Inquirer*, *Harrisburg Patriot-News*, *Boston Globe*, and the *Baltimore Sun*. He is the author of seven bestselling books on department-store histories and frequently serves as a consultant for various film, commercial, and educational projects. Lisicky resides in Baltimore, Maryland, where he is an oboist with the Baltimore Symphony Orchestra.

DISCOVER THOUSANDS OF LOCAL HISTORY BOOKS FEATURING MILLIONS OF VINTAGE IMAGES

Arcadia Publishing, the leading local history publisher in the United States, is committed to making history accessible and meaningful through publishing books that celebrate and preserve the heritage of America's people and places.

Find more books like this at
www.arcadiapublishing.com

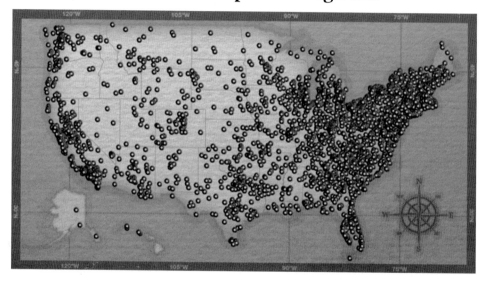

Search for your hometown history, your old stomping grounds, and even your favorite sports team.